The Secret Language of Feelings

A Rational Approach to Mastering Emotions

Calvin D. Banyan

Banyan Hypnosis Center for Training & Services, Inc.
Dallas, Texas, USA

To order copies of this book retail or wholesale, go
to www.hypnosiscenter.com or contact:

Banyan Hypnosis Center for Training & Services, Inc.
275 West Campbell Rd. Suite 245
North Dallas, Texas 75080
Tel: 469-969-2176

Published by Banyan Hypnosis Center for Training & Services, Inc.
Copyright 2003 by Calvin D. Banyan

All rights reserved under International and Pan-American
Copyright Conventions. Published in the United States by
Banyan Hypnosis Center for Training & Services, Inc.

Library of Congress Control Number: 2002095781

ISBN: 978-0-9712290-5-1

Cover design and graphics by Matt McKee
Manufactured in the United States of America

15 14

This book is dedicated to my mother, Arleen.

Mother, you were the first to hold me.
the first to teach me, and you always
loved me. Thank you, your eldest son.

Disclaimer

The Secret Language of Feelings was written to provide information regarding the nature of feelings and emotions. It is not designed to be a complete course in counseling, psychotherapy or psychology, or to offer medical advice. It is not meant to encompass all of the information available or needed to do any kind of therapeutic work. No single book could adequately prepare anyone for the practice of therapy or counseling.

This book was designed to help individuals wishing to help themselves. Implementation of the information in this book, when working with individuals carrying any kind of diagnosis of mental illness, should only be done under the guidance of an individual trained to work in those kinds of circumstances.

This book is sold with the understanding that the publisher and author are not engaged in rendering legal, accounting or other professional services beyond the scope of offering insight and understanding regarding the nature of feelings and emotions.

Furthermore, this book and its author do not in any way or fashion encourage any layperson or professional to engage in any practice or behavior that is illegal where he or she lives or works.

Every effort has been made to make this book as complete as possible given the nature of the topic. Much of this book contains information based on the experience of the author, who does not claim that each article of information has been empirically studied or proven. Doing so would preclude sharing this valuable information.

This book is for educational purposes only. The author and publisher shall have neither liability nor responsibility to any person or entity with respect to any loss or damage caused or alleged to be caused directly or indirectly by the information contained in this book.

If you do not wish to be bound by the above, you may return this book to the publisher for a full refund: Banyan Hypnosis Center for Training & Services, Inc., 275 West Campbell Rd., Suite 245, North Dallas, Texas 75080.

Acknowledgements

For many years, I have been sharing the information in *The Secret Language of Feelings* with my friends, clients and students. When I shared it with Samadhi Ishaya Wright, Ph.D., she inspired me to put it into book form for students of counseling and psychology.

I approached writing this book as if I were speaking to you as friends. That made the task enjoyable—but additional work was needed to turn my thoughts into the book you are holding today. I was assisted along the way by the wonderful people listed below.

For their invaluable suggestions, thanks to Samadhi Ishaya Wright, Ph.D.; Eric Robins, MD, co-author of "Your Hands Can Heal You;" Stephen C. Parkhill, author of "Answer Cancer, The Healing of a Nation," and Timothy Miller.

For writing a Foreword to the book, Samadhi Ishaya Wright, Ph.D.; Eric Robins, MD.

For cover design and grapics, Matt McKee. For polishing the manuscript, text design and typesetting, Carroll Morris. For preparing the manuscript for publication, editors Pamela Elias and Mary McCarty, indexer Rose M. Coad and production specialist Deb Desley.

Special thanks go to my dear wife Maureen Banyan, who inspires my understanding of feelings and emotions every day.

Foreword

Stress and negative emotions aren't just in the head, they are stored throughout the body. Many of us don't understand these emotions, and we don't like the way they feel. So we repress them, holding them deeply in the muscles, tissues and organs of the body, which makes us vulnerable to disease.

As a urologist in practice in the Los Angeles area, I see this happening all of the time. Many people are literally so cut off from their feelings that they are unable to realize their physical symptoms are actually emotions calling out to be heard, acknowledged and acted upon.

Calvin Banyan is a master hypnotist. Aside from running what is, in my opinion, the best hypnosis school in the country, Banyan understands emotions and how to transform them better than anyone I know. I had a session with him in September, 2002, and it was the single most powerful and positive experience of my life.

In "The Secret Language of Feelings," Banyan makes a call for people to begin reconnecting to their feelings and emotions, rather than cutting themselves off from them. In addition, he shows us how to interpret the language of feelings, so we can respond to them with positive actions that will enrich our lives.

I believe that the principles and practices in "The Secret Language of Feelings," will help many people reconnect not only with their emotions, but also with their bodies. When this happens—when emotions are embraced and their message heeded—a significant step is made forward in promoting optimal health and mental well-being.

Eric B. Robins, MD
Co-Author, "Your Hands Can Heal You"

This is one of those rare books that can be of benefit to almost anyone, because it is about something that unites us as human beings: emotions. However, Calvin Banyan looks at emotions and the feelings they generate from a new perspective — a perspective that, surprisingly, I never heard mentioned during many years of graduate school in psychology.

Banyan suggests that perhaps all of our feelings are useful, even good! I first heard him talk about this almost three years ago when I was fortunate to receive training from him in his 5-PATH process of hypnotherapy. I immediately began sharing the information with students in the college counseling courses I teach. I have delighted in the ease with which they assimilate this new knowledge and begin applying it in their lives. I hope the same will be true for all of you reading this book.

It is an exciting time to be alive. We are discovering more each day about who we are and our connection with the Source of Everything. Many people on a spiritual path have the mistaken belief that our emotions are to be denied or ignored, and that truly enlightened individuals would never experience something so "negative" as anger or sadness or fear. I would suggest that enlightenment means, in part, embracing the experience of being fully alive, in a human body that has a multitude of emotions flowing through it. A goal of spiritual/human evolution is to realize the gift present in the feelings experienced in every interaction or situation. The first step toward that goal is being willing to allow ourselves the experience of the situation — even when it feels nothing like a gift!

Grief, for example, is a strong emotion – one that can feel overwhelming in its intensity. Because of that, many people are not willing to experience it, choosing instead to deny it, repress the feelings associated with it, and distract themselves in any of the multitude of ways Banyan describes in this book. Both from my own personal life experiences and from my experiences as a hypnotherapist, I can testify to the incredible damage we inflict upon ourselves through this (unconscious) process.

Banyan does an excellent job of explaining how we have fallen into these unhealthy practices, and even more importantly, how very easy it can be to begin doing it differently today!

Samadhi Ishaya Wright, Ph.D.
Hypnotherapist and Educator
Lincoln, NE

Table of Contents

Part One:

Discovering the Secret Language

Introduction to Part One

This book reveals what people have wanted to know about the human condition from the very beginning of time: What are feelings for? Within its pages, you will discover the secret language of feelings. That language is a voice within us. Sometimes it is as soft as a whisper; sometimes it is as loud as a roar. It is an important voice, which, when fully understood, gives you a kind of guidance no other voice can.

The information in *The Secret Language of Feelings* was revealed during thousands of hours of working with hypnotherapy clients at the Banyan Hypnosis Center for Training and Services. It came from clients who spoke to us both in the normal waking state and in the state of hypnosis.

You do not need to undergo hypnotherapy in order to benefit from this book; however, it would make a perfect companion book for anyone involved in any therapy process.

The Secret Language of Feelings gives you a rational and reliable approach to understanding and responding to your feelings and emotions. It shows you how to create a more satisfying life, starting right now! You will learn how to overcome anger, guilt, frustration, sadness, loneliness and even "everyday" depression. You will better understand yourself, your family and the people you interact with on a daily basis.

In short, *The Secret Language of Feelings* offers the key to emotional rescue and beyond to happiness and success in life.

Chapter 1

The Secret Revealed

**The heart has its reasons
which reason does not know.**

-Blaise Pascal

Few secrets are kept for very long. Fewer secrets are kept for a lifetime. But this secret seems to have been kept throughout the history of the human race. It's a secret language that was never meant to be kept secret. It wasn't locked away in a cave and then uncovered by a shepherd boy or archeologists. This ancient set of truths, which make up an undeniably human code of instructions, has been buried inside every man, woman and child since there have been humans as we know them.

It's time now to reveal that which has been hidden. No pick and shovel uncovered this buried code. It was put together piece by piece while communicating directly with the subconscious minds of clients during thousands of hypnosis sessions. It was then verified by over two thousand clients who have used this information, along with other information from their hypnosis sessions, to better understand themselves and the people that they know and love. Since then, it's been taught to a limited number of hypnotherapists, counselors, psychologists, medical doctors, nurses and alternative medicine practitioners across the United States and around the world. Now it's offered to you.

This secret language of feelings is a discovery so powerful, and yet so obvious, that once you've learned it, you'll wonder why it wasn't revealed in such a simple and direct way many years ago. You may ponder how having learned it years earlier might have affected your life for the better. You may even come to the conclusion that young people who learn this universal language will undoubtedly grow up healthier mentally, physically, emotionally and socially than most adults today.

It's my belief that if the secret language of feelings were taught in our homes or in the schools, our children would be highly resistant to many of the temptations and behavior problems currently plaguing them. These informed children would grow up with wisdom and understanding far beyond their years. They'd also have a powerful tool to help them manage their feelings and avoid abusing of drugs, alcohol, tobacco, food and each other.

But there's also hope for those of us who have grown up without knowing the secret language of feelings. Indeed, hope is the great message of this book.

All Feelings Are Good

Our secret language of feelings reveals to us that all feelings are good! This concept lies at the foundation of learning the hidden language vibrating within us. The only "bad" feelings are the misunderstood feelings, and once you learn the language, you'll understand them. You'll learn their names and what they have to tell us. This new understanding will provide something that many people have longed for—a logical perspective on the experience of emotion. Too long we've thought of and treated emotions as illogical.

Once you learn to let your feelings and emotions speak to you, they'll teach you how to significantly reduce the level of anxiety and stress in your life. Comprehending the hidden language will also greatly increase your confidence and provide you with a new sense of direction.

Imagine having an internal voice moving you in the right direction, leading you to feel more satisfied with your life, because you're doing what is really right for you and the ones that you love. That would be a great shift for most of us, but it's exactly what this book can provide. People who feel their lives are meaningless will discover meaning as they read it. Those who already have a sense of purpose will find that their purpose will become clearer. They'll then be able to show others the way to find purpose and satisfaction in life.

The Discovery

Years of college failed to teach me the remarkable way in which the unconscious and subconscious levels of our mind struggles to communicate with us. It wasn't until I entered into the practice of hypnotherapy and had the opportunity to talk with clients who were in the state of hypnosis—where both subconscious and unconscious material is available—that I started to put things together.

As I began to understand the secret language of feelings and then teach it to my clients, the results were phenomenal. Clients began to take back control of their lives. They made significant progress with difficult issues such as addictions, obsessions and compulsions. They were able to lose weight and eliminate other self-defeating behaviors. They became generally happier and more confident and secure.

Be assured that you can get this kind of relief without the use of hypnosis if you follow the suggestions in this book. However, some people may find that meeting with a skilled hypnotherapist or learning a special kind of self-hypnosis called 7th Path™ helps them to benefit more rapidly and fully from knowledge of the secret language.

How Health Professionals Fail Us

If you asked your doctor, clergy, psychologist or counselor "What are vehicles for?," they'd probably answer, "To transport people and things from one place to another." If you asked them "What is a vacuum cleaner for?," they'd answer "To pick up dust and dirt." But if you were to ask them "What are feelings for?," they probably wouldn't have such a ready answer. Yet feelings have a purpose far more important in helping us create enjoyable and meaningful lives.

I believe the answer to the question "What are feelings for?" should be common knowledge to every helping professional, teacher, minister, manager and parent. Why? Because our feelings are nature's built-in guidance system. This system is designed to let us know which of our needs aren't being fulfilled and motivate us to take the actions necessary to fulfill them. When we ignore our feelings, our basic needs remain unmet. Our lives become filled with frustration and stress and eventually depression.

This is where psychology and medicine have let us down. Basically healthy individuals who have sought help because of feeling sad, mad or otherwise "bad" are routinely prescribed drugs, emotion-numbing medications that flatten out their lives, in the hope that they might be able to respond to issues and challenges without becoming emotional.

Adding chemicals to our bodies may make us feel better as long as we take them, but these drugs cure nothing. In fact, they blank out the very mechanism that nature created to help us recognize and satisfy our needs. In addition, the diagnoses we're given often become limiting labels and self-fulfilling prophesies of inadequacy. We may become emotionally, if not physically, addicted to the drugs. We may feel powerless and begin to believe that if we lack some chemical, we're handicapped.

At this point, how well we can do in our lives greatly depends (according to our medically manipulated beliefs) on the continuance of the prescribed drugs that we're encouraged to take, rather than on what we ourselves can do to move forward in self-understanding and personal growth. Well-meaning professionals then spend their valuable time with their clients encouraging them to stay on their "meds." Unfortunately, they're trained to believe that is the best they can do for their clients.

I'm not saying that medical intervention is never needed or advised. What I'm advocating is that before professionals make a diagnosis or prescribe a medication to alter the patient's experience of his or her own feelings, they should be able to quickly and confidently answer the simple and important question "What are feelings for?" If they can, they'll realize there are other steps that can be taken to restore the patient to a satisfying life.

Why We Bury Our Feelings

As you learn the secret language of feelings and begin to use it in your life, you'll learn how to greatly reduce feelings of stress, anger, sadness, loneliness, frustration and depression—without having to manage or suppress them in any dysfunctional or self-defeating way i.e., illegal drugs, alcohol, bad habits or addictions. You'll also begin to become aware of an internal guidance system that has always been there, but which society and perhaps your family taught you to ignore.

As a society, we have a long tradition of suppressing feelings. At the time when our country was being settled by frontiersmen and women, there was no assurance that an individual's needs could or would be fulfilled. Under the circumstances, it made little sense to complain of hardships, so those stoic men and women ignored the emotional pain they experienced and simply did what needed to be done. Such was also the case during The Great Depression and World War II.

The men and women of those times are our nation's heroes—strong, silent types who are held up as models, the people we look up to. With stoics as our accepted model, it's no wonder that from the time we were children we were made to feel bad, even guilty, for expressing anything other than quiet acceptance of any emotional pain that we found within ourselves. The only feeling that we were permitted to express was pleasure about what was going on around us. In some families, we were even cautioned not to be too happy or optimistic! After all, such positive thinking might only lead to disappointment.

Some of us have grown up in environments where expressing sadness or showing signs of anger or fear is punished. We've all experienced or witnessed a situation where a crying child is told by someone more powerful to "Shut up, or I'll give you something to cry about!" Immediately, the child is trained to stuff her feelings down to avoid punishment. As a result, she may end up denying having ever felt the pain. This kind of denial can lead to suppression or repression, resulting in emotional pressure that will eventually find a way to surface, usually in the form of addiction, obsession or compulsion.

Criticism and emotional abuse often follow when children express feelings that society says are "wrong." Boys are told that when they express sadness and cry, they're acting like little girls. Such criticism may lead to feelings of inadequacy and shame. Then those feelings are also squelched.

Girls are told that expressing feelings of anger is unattractive. If girls express their dissatisfaction, they're told that they aren't feminine. They can be cast out of social groups when they don't acquiesce to unfair situations, thereby being taught only to show feelings that are "acceptable" for girls, such as sadness—but not too much sadness. Too much sadness can lead to crying, which also may not be allowed. Girls may even be accused of crying only to manipulate those around them. Thus it seems that for both boys and girls, exhibiting feelings is a losing situation.

Both children and adults are even told that it's immoral to experience feeling "bad." This is especially true if we feel angry. Furthermore, our society tells us that we're ill if we become depressed. Again, we bury these feelings and deny ever having felt them in an effort to appear normal.

Coping Through Distraction

Given the above, it's not surprising that as children, we have a tendency to handle our emotions by just pretending that we don't feel bad. Children are also good at forgetting the events that have caused the emotions as a way of coping with them. This forgetting and pretending provides some temporary relief, but the memories of those experiences are stored in our subconscious minds, along with the emotions attached to them.

As adults, we need to develop a coping strategy which is more effective than the pretending and forgetting strategies of the child. If we don't develop one, we'll have to cope with all of the old emotions of childhood piled up inside of us, as well as the new, unsatisfied emotions of the present.

Typically, we handle our emotions through a process of distracting, by focusing our attention on something else besides the feeling—something like food, alcohol or drugs. But there's a better way.

Emotion is pure motivation.
It's a psychological pressure to act.

Chapter 2

How Feelings Affect Us

When I use the term "feelings" I'm talking about how our emotions make us feel, the physical expression of the emotions inside us. Emotions are generated in our subconscious minds, while the physiological changes—feelings—that we associate with those emotions are generated by our unconscious mind. Let me explain further.

As a hypnotherapist, I've learned to think about the conscious, subconscious and unconscious levels of the mind as having particular attributes and functions. The conscious mind is the smallest of the three levels. It contains only what we're focusing on at any given time. This is a small quantity of things; research suggests that our conscious mind can only hold about seven to nine individual pieces of information at any given time. The conscious mind is good at analyzing these few items and can be quite logical, given enough training and information. We call this being rational.

The subconscious mind, in contrast, is a vast database of information. It contains the sum of all of our experiences and beliefs, and it generates emotional responses according to our past experiences, beliefs and expectations about the future.

The unconscious mind isn't really unconscious—we're just not conscious of its ongoing work. The unconscious mind keeps our bodies working and responding to the outside world. It regulates autonomic body functions such as breathing and generally manages all of our organs. It's also the part of us that changes the emotions generated in the subconscious mind into feelings.

The unconscious mind, then, creates all of the physiological phenomena associated with each emotion. When we experience the emotion called fear, it releases adrenaline into our bodies, causing us to feel all of the responses we associate with fear, such as muscle tension and increased heart rate. When we're sad, it generates our tears and the ache in our hearts. In short, it translates our emotional states into physical feelings, which explains why we refer to our emotions as *feelings.*

Emotion results from our experiences and from the meanings and perceptions we associate with those experiences. **Emotion is pure motivation. It's a psychological pressure to act.** When we suppress our feelings, we're suppressing this motivation, this pressure inside of us.

We suppress our feelings by directing our attention away from what is bothering us to something else, usually something that we find pleasant or have found to be pleasant in the past. An example is the common behavior of feeling down and then eating. Other people may feel bad and distract themselves with television, a movie, a drink, or even prescription and non-prescription drugs.

Learning and using the secret language of feelings takes you out of this rut of habitual behavior or addictions. You'll have the understanding you need to behave in ways that are much more satisfying than living a life of coping through the use of distractors.

Why Little Things Hurt a Lot

All of us have over-reacted to a situation. All of a sudden, we feel like whatever is happening is just too much. It's the last straw, the proverbial straw that broke the camel's back. Such over-reactions tend to happen when something causes us to experience an unpleasant feeling such as anger or fear, only we experience it much more powerfully than can be justified by the situation.

Jerry (it could just as easily be Jenny) is working on a project when his boss (or spouse or child) makes a request. It's really not that big of a deal, but for some reason, it lands like an unreasonable demand. Maybe Jerry is already under stress from previous commitments and doesn't have the time. Maybe he feels everyone else's needs always come first. Or maybe he's simply tired or headachy. Whatever the reason, Jerry finds himself reacting totally out of proportion to the request. He blows up, says hurtful things that he will later regret and storms out of the room.

After he cools down, Jerry realizes he has just acted like a 5-year-old throwing a tantrum. He tries to justify his behavior, perhaps by blaming others, but deep down, he actually feels embarrassed and confused as to why he responded in such an extreme way. He wishes he could be calmer and more patient in such situations. He's promised himself he will be, but every so often, his emotions erupt and he ends up totally out of control.

Jerry knows he's getting the reputation of having a bad temper. He realizes that his problem is getting worse, not better. He's afraid of what might happen next—he even fears that he might lose control and hurt someone. He doesn't even want to contemplate what that would lead to.

An explanation for over-reactions such as Jerry's lies in a principle that I call "emotional resonance." In the study of physics or acoustics, we learn that all things resonate, or in other words, vibrate. They have what is called a resonate frequency, a point at which they're able to vibrate easily. At this point of resonance, they become energized.

For example, if a piano and a guitar were tuned to each other and then placed in the same room, I could go over to the piano and strike the A key with sufficient force to cause the A string on the guitar to vibrate. The sound that the piano made, the A note, would move through the air—an acoustic vibration—sympathetically activating the A string on the guitar.

How Feelings Affect Us

How this happens is no mystery, it's just physics! The principle of sympathetic resonance states that all things have some frequency at which they will vibrate sympathetically if a similar vibration (energy) is generated.

Sympathetic resonance is also the reason why an electric guitar on stage but not in use during a musical performance must be turned off. If it isn't, the music being performed will cause the strings to vibrate. The guitar begins to screech, making a feedback sound similar to the one that a microphone can make.

Emotional resonance operates in much the same way. An event in the present has a certain emotional vibration. It can cause the sympathetic vibration of a memory with similar emotional content. Here's how that happens.

Our nervous system is made up of water, minerals, proteins, fats and so on. When we're in a particular emotional state, there are changes in our physiology that can be measured—changes in muscle tension, heart rate and brain wave frequencies, just to name a few. Each time this occurs, the changes are stored in the subconscious and unconscious mind, along with all of our other memories.

This is the mechanism by which emotions from the past come to be stored in the nervous system, in the unconscious and subconscious levels of the mind and perhaps even in other tissues of our body—any place where there are nerves. These stored emotions can be recalled in an instant when something occurs that we associate with them.

Stated in another way, memories and emotions from the past are activated when a current event resonates with them. For example, if you were driving down the road and an old song came on the radio, just hearing it would bring up memories of the past with no conscious effort on your part. Perhaps you'd have flashes of an old relationship or of a specific time in your life such as a vacation. Your memories might even contain the emotions and feelings associated with them.

The subconscious and unconscious levels of our minds, where our memories and emotions are stored and our feelings are generated, are highly organized. They respond easily to what's going on around us, activating memories and associated emotions by resonating with them.

Emotional resonance explains what happened to Jerry when he over-reacted to a request. For Jerry, something about the request being made or the person making it—or both—resonated with stuffed emotions of the past, causing them to become activated. They then cascaded into the present, carrying with them behaviors associated with an earlier time, perhaps when he really was a 5-year-old! As a result, Jerry ended up acting like a child, becoming temporarily out of control.

Learning how to respond to the information in the secret language of feelings will give you a very effective tool for dissolving the old pent-up emotions from the past. When they're gone, the old feelings that once resonated and cascaded into the present will also be gone, and the cycle of over-reacting will end.

It's important to recognize that dissolving the pent-up emotions and feelings doesn't mean that you'll lose your memory of the past. As hurtful feelings change or fade away, your personal history will become mere information, devoid of emotional charge. As a result, you'll be much more in control. People will marvel at the change in you as you become more patient and calm in situations that would have previously caused you to "blow your top." Best of all, you'll like yourself much more!

Internal and External Stress

As we go through life, we constantly experience two different sources of stress: internal and external stress. Internal stress consists of all of the old emotions of the past as discussed above. It's sealed within our nervous systems, always there, whether we're aware of it or not. External stress is mostly caused by our emotional response to the demands that life puts upon us, such as work, school and relationships. Internal stress and external stress are always combining to create the level of stress that we're experiencing at any moment.

Many philosophies and faiths from around the world encourage us to live in the moment, in "The Now." When we live in "The Now," as these philosophies and faiths describe it, we're completely free from internal stress caused by a build-up from the past. We're also free from problems experienced because of emotional resonance with pent-up emotions from the past. We're calmer, our perceptions are more accurate and our decisions are more satisfying.

For those whose experience of the present is uncomfortable due to internal and external stress, learning to live in "The Now" seems like an unreachable ideal. But once you begin using your internal guidance system, the secret language of feelings, you'll experience a reduction in your level of stress. Life will become more pleasant, and you'll actually begin to experience moments of being simply aware of what is, of living in "The Now."

Stress and the Weakest Link

To illustrate how harmful this interaction of internal stress and external stress is, imagine for a moment a chain with its links stretched out horizontally. If stress or tension is applied to both ends, the weakest link begins to open, compromising the strength of the whole chain.

In this illustration, the chain represents your genetic code. If you were to look at your chromosomes you'd see that they look like a chain. Now imagine that each one of the links in the chain represents some physical aspect of your body. One link in the chain represents your hair. Others represent your skin, liver, stomach, immune system and so forth.

Everyone's body has its own relative strengths and weaknesses. Some people have smooth, glowing skin and others have thick, shiny hair. Some people have strong stomachs. It seems they can eat anything and it doesn't bother them, while others must be very careful about what they eat.

Internal Stress ← 〰〰〰〰〰〰 → **External Stress**

Figure 1: How stress affects our bodies

Your body reveals its particular weaknesses when you're experiencing stress, the way a weak link in a chain opens up when the chain is stressed by being pulled from both ends. Some people respond to stress by getting headaches, others may experience skin problems, while still others may lose the ability to concentrate or remember.

If the stress is temporary, the effects can also be temporary. When I was going through a particularly stressful part of graduate school, for example, my back began to hurt and my vision became blurry. But after the stress had passed, these problems subsided.

Chronic stress, on the other hand, can lead to serious health problems such as a depleted immune system, hypertension, heart attack, stroke and even death. That's why it's so important for us to handle our stressors in a better way than merely coping with them or distracting ourselves from them.

Our bodies respond immediately when the level of stress is reduced. To illustrate, let's say the chain in our example is being stressed by having tension applied on both ends. What would happen if we removed the stress from even one end? It would go limp. If there were a weak link starting to give way, it would close up again. In the same way, as you remove this stress from your system, your body is better able to heal and protect itself from disease.

The Seething Cauldron

Internal stress is a major factor in both emotional and physical health. To illustrate just how intense our internal stress can be at any given moment, I use a model I call "The Seething Cauldron of Emotions." Understanding this model can help you understand how—and why—you feel "good" or "bad."

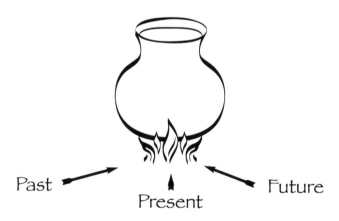

Figure 2: The Seething Cauldron of Emotions

How Feelings Affect Us

In this illustration, your emotional state at any given time is represented by how hot or cold the contents of the cauldron are. As the contents heat up, you experience increasing emotional pressure and discomfort. As the contents cool down, you begin to experience a state of peace, calm and relaxation.

As you can see, the cauldron has a small flame at the bottom of it. This flame keeps the contents of the cauldron continually seething, because it's fed by three fuel sources. One fuel source is your past, the second is your present set of circumstances, and the third is your future. All three are able to feed the flame at any one time, because all three can generate emotion.

As stated previously, you carry all of your experiences and emotions from the past within you. They're contained in your nervous system and subconscious mind, ready to be activated by circumstances that are similar in emotion or mood. So even when there's nothing bothering you in the present, the cauldron and its contents—your internal state—never really cool down unless you have adequately resolved the issues from your past. Any unresolved feelings of anger, grief, fear and inadequacy are there, providing fuel for the flame.

Under the cauldron on the right is the fuel source that we call the future. If you're concerned about anything that's going to happen, or might happen, your concern provides more emotional fuel for the flame, which heats the cauldron up. For example, if you're a person who dreads giving a speech and you have to give one next week, you'll begin to feel anxious about it long before the event occurs. You'll continue to feel more and more nervous right up to the moment that you give the speech.

Some people experience this kind of anxiety all the time, even though there's no real threat in their present or future. In their case, the anxiety is chronic and the ongoing stress is constantly feeding the flame under the cauldron. ***Chronic anxiety can cause all kinds of problems—it can even create an imbalance in brain chemicals due to the constant release of the chemicals generated by fear, such as adrenaline.***

This example shows how chronic stress can lead to chemical imbalances that medications would seem to balance. When the drugs make you feel better, doctors and drug manufacturing companies come to the conclusion that the problem is a chemical imbalance that the drugs seem to successfully address. And they'd be partially right.

They'd be wrong, however, if they thought that the imbalance was caused by the nervous system being diseased or genetically deficient. In the case of chronic anxiety, the cause isn't physical, but rather the result of poor education or negative life experiences leading to a habit of fearful thinking.

Now let's return to our Seething Cauldron. With unresolved issues from the past adding fuel for the flame and worries about the future providing yet more fuel, it's easy to see that even when nothing particularly challenging is going on in the present, you still cannot be completely stress-free in the moment. Your cauldron is already seething. Then, when some little but significant thing comes up in the present, you simply boil over, becoming overly stressed, angry, frustrated or depressed.

When you boil over, so to speak, you'll be driven to find some way to cope with your painful emotions. You'll feel as if you have no other alternative but to seek out drugs to flatten your mood or find comfort in some kind of distracting activity like eating, working, or just plain busying yourself with activities.

Living in "the Now"

All is not hopeless, however. Through implementing what you're beginning to learn, you'll be able to remove excess fuel (emotion) from your past and automatically eliminate chronic worry about the future.

It's worth noting that the future event you perceive as causing your stress isn't really causing it! The thoughts you're having about the future event are creating emotions that resonate with similar events in your past. This emotional resonance causes a cascade of powerful feelings from the past into your present, which in turn causes an over-reaction to the upcoming event.

In the vast majority of cases, when we're worried about the future, we're really living in the past. In our example of worrying about having to give a speech, the worry is generated by negative emotions from the past, emotions held in the nervous system relating to fearful or embarrassing experiences of public speaking.

This explains the fact that when we dissolve away painful emotions of the past, we simultaneously and automatically rid ourselves of excessive worrying about the future! When the emotions of the past are removed from our nervous systems, upcoming or present situations cannot resonate with them, because they're no longer there. We feel much more peaceful, calm and in control.

When past and future fuel sources are reduced or eliminated, there's only one fuel source left to affect your cauldron—whatever is happening in the present. As a result, the cauldron cools, and a cool pot is slow to boil. It takes a lot more to get you upset. You become more patient. You think more clearly. Your perceptions become more accurate, and even your memory is likely to improve. You can begin to experience the freedom of truly living in "The Now."

Chapter 3

What Our Feelings Tell Us

What are feelings for? Why are they all good? Fortunately, the answer is very simple. ***All feelings are good, because their purpose is to provide us with information, direction and motivation that will help us create a satisfying life.***

Our feelings are a product of our internal wisdom, which is attempting to guide us and motivate us to satisfy our needs, wants and desires. Satisfying needs, wants and desires—especially our needs—is necessary in order to take good care of ourselves and those we love, as well as provide for the survival of our species, humankind.

Our feelings are designed to motivate us by providing us with an experience of either satisfaction or discomfort. The amount of discomfort generated by unmet needs depends upon whether or not we take actions to satisfy them. If we don't or can't take satisfying actions, the discomfort can become extreme over time—even painful.

Helpful Definitions

Before going on to the core of this chapter, let's establish the definitions we'll be working with. From this point on, when I use the term "bad" in regard to feelings, I simply mean that you're experiencing feelings of discomfort or pain. "Bad" isn't a moral judgment. Although uncomfortable or painful feelings might seem to be "bad," their function is positive—to provide you with necessary information and motivation. Seen in this light, they're actually "good."

When I use the term "good" to describe feelings, I'm referring to feelings or emotions that are pleasurable. Good feelings are the experience of sensations associated with being safe and having other needs, wants or desires satisfied. They include feelings like safety, security, happiness, joy, achievement and love.

As noted above, feelings of discomfort, the so-called "bad" feelings, are generated when you're not fulfilling your needs, wants or desires. They include sadness, fear, loneliness, anger and guilt. When you feel them, begin to listen to them. They're attempting to communicate with you. They each have a specific message related to a specific need, want or desire.

Needs, Wants and Desires

The painful feelings that we experience are generated within us in order to motivate us to live productive and satisfying lives, to do the sometimes difficult things necessary in order to satisfy our needs, wants and desires. They also motivate us to do what's necessary for the survival of our species. But what are these needs, wants and desires? Where do they come from?

The term "needs" can be defined as those things we must have to be healthy and to survive either as individuals or as a species. Human needs are built into our genetic code. They've been passed down from one generation to the next, modified only through slow adaptation to changes in the environment. The motivation to fulfill these "must haves" is also genetically programmed into us.

Basic human needs include food, water, shelter and safety. When these needs are met, we feel safe. We can then turn our attention to other needs that make us feel secure and promote the propagation of the species, such as relationships which result in children, families and communities. Satisfying human needs is necessary for both individuals and social groups.

Every human being has the same needs. "Wants," on the other hand, vary considerably from culture to culture and from person to person. They also can change a great deal over time as an individual moves from childhood into the teenage years, on to adulthood and finally to older adulthood.

Individuals from different cultures and environments learn to value things differently. In one culture, drinking a glass of wine each day may be regarded as a healthy thing to do. It can even be considered mandatory in some religions for ceremonial purposes. Yet in other cultures, drinking a glass of wine may be considered grounds for a wide range of punishments, even removal from the society.

While basic needs are common to all human beings and wants can be common to a culture or group, desires are very individual. When I refer to "desires," I mean things we feel that we need or want very strongly. There's an element of passion in the experience of desire.

For the most part, people living in our society have their fundamental needs met. Few of you who are reading this book are in a state of fear about where your next meal is coming from or where you're going to sleep tonight. When it comes to unmet needs, the discomfort most of us feel is due to dissatisfaction associated with self-worth, relationships or level of achievement.

Since our needs are by and large satisfied, most of us can focus on our wants and desires. However, satisfying our wants isn't as easy as might be imagined. What we want—or think we want—can be easily manipulated by the ongoing stream of commercials and advertisements, each announcing some item that we're encouraged to want, such as a new model of car or some new style of clothing.

Marketers constantly pair images representing our basic needs with items they want us to purchase. This creates the impression that if we purchase the items, we will be able to satisfy those needs.

or desires. For example, an expensive car is shown with a successful-looking man or woman at the wheel, or a particular brand of clothing is shown worn by sexually attractive models.

Desires, as mentioned above, are highly individual and arise from a deep place within us. As defined for this discussion, they're positive motivations, urging us toward exploring and developing our talents, pointing us toward our unique calling in life and showing us how we can contribute and make a difference.

History, literature and daily life provide us with examples of how needs, wants and desires can be misinterpreted or misdirected, and how the means taken to fulfill them can be harmful to self and others. The focus in this book is to show how we can become adept at identifying our real needs, wants and desires and creating a strategy for fulfilling them in a *satisfying* way, which by implication also means a way that's positive for us and harmless to those around us.

Signals from the Secret Language

Now that we've established the terms we'll be using, let's have some fun using a metaphor to describe how our feelings are signals that can provide us with the information we need to take care of ourselves appropriately.

Signals are a form of communication. When properly understood, they provide us with beneficial information. For example, if you're driving your car and you want to communicate to other drivers that you intend to make a turn, you use the turn signal. When the other drivers see the signal, they can respond to it in a way that keeps both them and you safe.

Feelings can also lead to beneficial responses when properly understood. They're signals indicating that you're either fulfilling or not fulfilling your needs, wants, and desires. Feeling good is a signal that the actions you have taken to satisfy your needs have been successful. **Feeling bad is a signal that some need is unmet. It's a call to take the action necessary to satisfy the need.**

This new understanding of feelings can provide you with direction leading to a satisfying response. A satisfying response is the action you can take to fulfill the need, thus causing a reduction or elimination of the painful experience of emotion, i.e., fear, anger, guilt, etc. When you understand that "bad" or painful feelings are giving you necessary information, you move beyond managing them to actually using them in a beneficial way and ultimately removing them by removing their cause.

When we satisfy our need for food, we experience a sense of well-being. We don't feel hungry again in just a few minutes; the sense of satisfaction lasts for hours, until our body again signals that it needs nourishment. Satisfying our emotional needs is like satisfying our hunger. Our sense of well-being isn't fleeting—it may last a few days or weeks or even months. However, as life goes on and our circumstances change, the state of our needs changes. The need that was satisfied begins once again to exert pressure for attention and action. This is the rhythm, the driving force behind the dance of life.

Now to our metaphor. A car has basic needs, such as the need for oil or gas, that must be attended to in order to keep it running in a reliable way. To ensure that these needs are addressed, cars are equipped with indicator lights that go on when there's an action the driver needs to take.

For example, a car needs oil to function reliably. When the oil gets low, the indicator light on the car's dashboard alerts the driver, so that she can take the appropriate action of filling the oil reservoir. (Author's note: I use "she" as the universal pronoun throughout this book, to avoid the awkward "he or she" and the plural "they.")

We're like the car—we also have needs that must be satisfied in order to function optimally. Our feelings indicate what need is calling for attention, just like the lights and gauges on the dashboard of a car alert us to what the car needs.

How We Distract from our Feelings

All of us would no doubt go immediately to the next filling station if the oil light flashed on while we were driving our car. We aren't so quick to identify what action to take when it comes to fulfilling our own needs, however. We all too often resort to a behavior I call "distracting." That is, instead of taking direct action to fulfill the need, we do something that makes us feel momentarily better, but doesn't address the need.

To illustrate, let's say I'm driving along and the oil light goes on. I immediately know something's wrong, and I start feeling bad. In this case, the bad feeling is called "worried." The oil light isn't bad, however. It's just a signal telling me there's something that needs to be addressed.

But what if I didn't know what it meant when the oil light flashed on? I would experience the distress of seeing a bright indicator light, but I wouldn't know what to do about it. So I might try to ignore it. I could try to distract myself from it by turning on the radio. Or, if one of my coping strategies was eating, I might pull into the first Dairy Queen or other fast food restaurant. If I did stop at the Dairy Queen, I'd soon be riding along in my car with the oil light still on, eating an ice cream cone and thinking, "That was the right thing to do. I feel a lot better now!"

But what has that action really accomplished when it comes to the message of the indicator light? Nothing. I've managed to make myself feel temporarily better by distracting myself with something that I enjoy, in this case, the pleasant sensation of eating my ice cream cone. But when I'm finished with my sweet and creamy distractor, my attention is called back to the oil light. The distress of the situation returns to my awareness and I mutter, "Boy, that darn light is annoying!" The message of the flashing light remains unheard.

The problem with distractors and all kinds of distracting—but ultimately unsatisfying behaviors—is this: Distractors are useful to some extent, even if only temporarily so. The ice cream did make me feel better for a while. My stress level went down significantly. Because of that, I might think about getting another ice cream cone. If I do, I've begun the habit of distraction, which could turn into ice cream addiction. If I continued this pattern, I might even become emotionally dependent on the ice cream.

That might not sound like such a bad thing, but what if I decided to distract myself by seeking out the nearest tavern? I could go in, order a drink and maybe have a cigarette. Sure enough, I 'd soon be thinking, "This is much better." Distracting myself with alcohol and cigarettes could become my addiction, driven by emotional dependence. ***By emotional dependence, I mean the pattern of relying on a distractor in order to cope with the painful experience of emotion, rather than satisfying the need, want or desire the emotion points to.***

The problems with the feel bad/distract scenario are many. The most obvious are the negative effects of addictions to substances (food, tobacco, alcohol, etc.) or behaviors (TV, shopping, pornography, etc.). The least obvious but perhaps greatest concern is that when you habitually indulge in these distractors, you'll probably be leaving important needs, wants and desires unfulfilled. This isn't good for you, society or humankind in general.

Now let's go back to the time in the example when I first noticed the oil light. Thankfully, oil lights have the word "oil" on or next to them. Without this label, they would just be a nuisance. But because they're named, they become signals, providing us with information that we can use immediately.

Most of you don't go into distraction mode when the oil light in our car goes on, because you know what it means and you know what to do. You stop at a gas station to check the oil yourself or have someone check it for you. If the oil level is low, you buy some and fill up the reservoir.

In either case, the action taken fills the need that the car has for oil. When you take care of a need, even a car's need, it leads to a feeling of satisfaction. When you see the indicator light go out, you know that you have acted responsibly and effectively. This kind of response leads to further confidence in operating the car, and you feel sure that you can handle this kind of situation if it comes up again.

Obviously this is a much better choice than distracting, which does not take care of the cause of the problem. ***Taking action to satisfy a need not only removes the cause of the problem, it avoids all of the side effects of distraction, such as weight gain and alcohol dependence.***

Emotional Eating

Distracting ourselves from painful feelings by eating is one of the most common problems in our society. This kind of distraction is called emotional eating. It contributes to obesity, which is one of the greatest health risks of modern American society.

Emotional eating occurs when someone eats in response to a

feeling—boredom, anxiety, frustration or depression—rather than in response to true physical hunger or needs. People who have trouble controlling their weight often eat before they experience real physical hunger. They may have even forgotten what it feels like and therefore don't have a way to differentiate between real physical hunger and emotional hunger. Here are a couple of helpful suggestions that will help you tell the difference.

First, physical hunger isn't picky. It doesn't care if you eat a balanced healthy meal or pure junk food—a salad or a hamburger and fries will satisfy it equally well! Real physical hunger is a physical discomfort that fades as soon as you get a sufficient quantity of food in your stomach. It will even stop temporarily if you just fill up your stomach with water.

Second, many people are surprised to find out that real physical hunger resides in a specific location in their body. When I ask my weight-loss clients where they feel their hunger, they most often point to the lower part of their abdomen around the navel. They're then surprised to find out that the location they're pointing to isn't their stomach, but rather their small intestines or "gut." I use the word "gut" because most of us have heard the expression of, "I had a real gut reaction." When you feel a strong discomfort in that area, a kind of "gut reaction," you're not experiencing physical hunger. That "gut reaction" is a feeling—a physical response to emotion.

Real physical hunger, on the other hand, occurs in the stomach, a few inches up from the gut. To locate your stomach, find the bottom edge of your sternum (the boney part at the center of your chest). The edge of your sternum covers the top third of your stomach.

After losing the excess weight, many of our clients attribute a great deal of their success to learning how to check for real physical hunger. When they realize they're not feeling physical hunger, they can ask themselves, "What am I really feeling? Am I tired, bored, lonely or frustrated?" Once they've identified what they're feeling, they can respond in a satisfying way.

Emotional eating looks quite different from eating due to physical hunger, as you'll see in the example of Magalina. Magalina is a typical weight-loss client. One of her main problems is that she snacks at home in the evenings. Sitting at home with nothing to do, Magalina gets a feeling and thinks, "I'm craving something."

As the process of distraction begins, Magalina automatically assumes she's craving food. She wanders into the kitchen, wondering what will satisfy her hunger. First she eats some cookies, but they don't satisfy her. Then she eats some potato chips, thinking that something salty will do the trick. When that doesn't fill her need, she remembers the leftovers from the night before. They tasted so good then, they must be the answer. Still unsatisfied, she tops it all off with a bowl of ice cream. In the end, she's stuffed to the point of being uncomfortable, she's more frustrated than ever—and she's still craving something!

What Our Feelings Tell Us

As you can see, Magalina's cravings aren't real hunger. Remember, anytime you think or say "I'm craving something" you're actually saying, "I'm thinking of trying to satisfy a feeling by distracting myself with food." Once you realize your feelings are trying to help you do something more satisfying than eat, you'll find it easy to avoid emotional eating.

Drinking, taking drugs, working too much—*doing anything too much to distract from feeling bad*—is unhealthy behavior. And, believe it or not, it can be stopped without any feelings of deprivation, because those distractors are ultimately frustrating, not satisfying. ***Only the satisfying response—taking the action necessary to fill a need—can truly meet your emotional need.*** This response is what your feelings are trying to get you to do, and learning the secret language of feelings will show you how.

As previously mentioned, the problem of distracting ourselves from our feelings is greater than the side effects that drinking, shopping, watching TV, working too much or taking drugs can cause in our lives. The greater, underlying problem is that the message of the feelings—that our needs, wants or desires need attending to—is left unaddressed and unsatisfied. The result can be a pattern of distraction leading to addiction and ultimately a life sadly lacking in satisfaction, devoid of real happiness and joy.

Using the Secret Language of Feelings helps you break the cycle of frustration and depression, allowing you to create a more satisfying life.

Chapter 4

The Feel Bad/Distract Cycle

Remember that feelings are like the lights and gauges on the dashboard of a car. When you feel bad, it's because you aren't fulfilling a need, want or desire. If you don't understand the language of your feelings, it's like driving a car with all of the lights and gauges on the dashboard written in a foreign language! You're left with only the discomfort of the light turning on or the gauge going into the red zone. You experience the urge to do something, but you don't know what.

This is similar to the "craving" that Magalina experienced in our earlier example. She felt motivated, but she didn't know how to use that motivation in a way that would satisfy the cause of the feelings. So she fell into her habit of distracting with food. That's why *naming the feeling is a very important first step in learning the vocabulary of the secret language.*

Three Categories of Feelings

In the secret language of feelings, we identify three separate categories of feelings. I call the first level Primary Feelings. *Primary Feelings are exactly equivalent to the lights on the dashboard of a car.* They're experienced as soon as some need, want or desire in your life becomes significantly unsatisfied. We experience Primary Feelings as being uncomfortable, and they can become increasingly painful if the need is left unsatisfied.

Here is a quick example. If you aren't in a significant relationship, and you've been without any kind of significant relationship for some time, you'll begin to feel lonely. Loneliness is the painful feeling associated with not satisfying the need for human companionship and association.

If you don't fill that need, the loneliness will continue. You can distract using every means imaginable, but when you get done with the distractor, you return to the pain of loneliness. Distractors don't work because they don't fulfill the need. They're self-reinforcing, however, because they make you feel better in the short term.

A first step toward understanding the futility of distractors is to examine the effectiveness of the behavior by asking questions like these:

How much do I have to eat until I have a satisfying relationship?
How much do I have to drink until I have a satisfying relationship?
How much do I have to work until I have a satisfying relationship?

How much do I have to shop until I have a satisfying relationship?
How much TV do I have to watch until I have a satisfying relationship?
How many times do I have to blame others until I have a satisfying relationship?

As you read those questions, you might have been thinking, "That doesn't make any sense!"

That's right! The questions themselves are illogical, so they reveal the illogical association between the need and the distracting behavior. Distracting behaviors (eating, drinking, blaming, etc.) aren't related to the issue which is causing the Primary Feeling. For example, none of the distractors listed above can satisfy the need for having a good relationship.

The Feel Bad/Distract Cycle

Unfortunately, many people find themselves caught in the trap of feeling bad and then distracting themselves from the feeling. The cycle could look like the figure below.

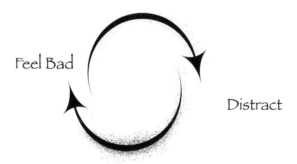

Feel Bad

Distract

Figure 3: The Feel Bad/Distract Cycle

Adding Frustration

The feel bad/distract cycle leads to frustration. The distractor does not satisfy the need, but because doing it offers temporary relief, you do it again when you find yourself feeling bad. As a result, the need remains unsatisfied.

In our example above, the need was for relationships. If you continue to attempt to fulfill the need without success—either by acting in a way you expect would cause you to meet someone, such as getting out of the house and socializing, or by distracting—a new

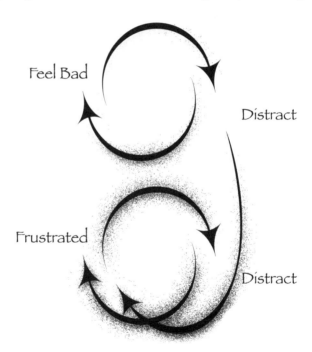

Figure 4: The Feel Bad/Distract/Frustrated Cycle

painful feeling will emerge. This new emotional pain is frustration. Frustration is always secondary to some other painful emotion you've been feeling. That is why I call it the Secondary Feeling.

You never feel frustrated unless you're first experiencing a Primary Feeling. **When you're unsuccessful in satisfying the need, want or desire associated with that feeling, you'll increase the pain by adding the Secondary Feeling of frustration.** Initially, you were lonely. After a period of trying unsuccessfully to satisfy the need for a relationship, you moved to the next part of the cycle. You became lonely and frustrated. This part of the cycle is shown in Figure 4.

Frustration can be felt in conjunction with any other feeling except the Tertiary Feeling of depression, which we'll discuss next. For example, you might have experienced feeling:

Lonely and frustrated
Sad and frustrated
Angry and frustrated
Bored and frustrated
Worried and frustrated

If you're able to take an action that satisfies the Primary Feeling, both the Primary Feeling and the frustration will fade away. **However, if your efforts to satisfy the Primary Feeling are continually unsuccessful, your feeling of frustration will continually increase.** You'll become more and more intensely frustrated.

The distraction/frustration cycle goes nowhere but downward toward depression. As the pain of an unsatisfied need increases, the frustration related to unsuccessful behavior intensifies, which is in turn experienced as a greater drive to distract. Thus, the cravings or urges become stronger and more compelling.

Also, when you use distractors, whatever relief you experience is temporary, making you feel better only while you're in the act of distracting. When you finish the distracting behavior, the urge to distract will return even more strongly. This is one of the great differences between distractors and satisfying responses. When you respond to a Primary Feeling with a satisfying response, the cause of the feeling is removed or reduced. This is experienced as a reduction or elimination of the urge to act. The motivation experienced as pain fades away until the need becomes unsatisfied once again.

Most importantly, when the motivation returns after a period of satisfaction, the urge will NOT be stronger than before. In fact, it may be less intense, because you'll know how to respond to it more quickly. You can actually respond to the feeling before it becomes so strong that you resort to distraction. For example, if you were lonely, you could simply call a friend and visit for a while, perhaps making plans for the weekend. That would be a satisfying response.

Adding Depression

Everything is different when you're caught in the cycle of distraction. Without a pattern of satisfying responses, you tend to ignore the unpleasant Primary Feeling at first. This is because you don't really understand what to do with it. You will, generally, allow it to become more intense and thus more painful, because you don't like the side effects of the distracting behavior, i.e., gaining weight, having a smoker's cough, experiencing problems associated with alcohol or drug abuse, etc. Eventually, when the pain becomes strong enough, you begin the distracting behavior.

This leaves the Primary Feeling unsatisfied, and when the Primary feeling is unsatisfied, you become frustrated. As the frustration continues to grow in intensity, it can become unhealthy. Remember, all of these unsatisfied feelings are a source of stress to your body, not to mention your relationships and work life. This leads us to probably the most misunderstood level of emotions, depression.

As you become more and more frustrated, you can go beyond feeling like a seething, or even boiling, cauldron of emotions. You begin to feel like a pressure cooker, straining to keep a lid on all of that built-up frustration! This is a very unhealthy state to be in. But you have a built-in safety valve. ***When frustration reaches its upper limits, and you're about to explode or experience a meltdown, the Tertiary Feeling of Depression kicks in.***

Now, your mind and body start sending you a totally different signal—they tell you to quit trying, to give up, that it's useless. You begin to feel hopeless, a feeling that is also known as depression. Depression is there to save you from exploding or having a mental and physical meltdown. It's nature's way of saying that you need a break and you need it now.

Let me put this all together. Primary feelings are designed to tell you that you aren't fulfilling an important need, want or desire. The Secondary Feeling of frustration tells you that what you're doing is not working. It's a call for a change in your approach to

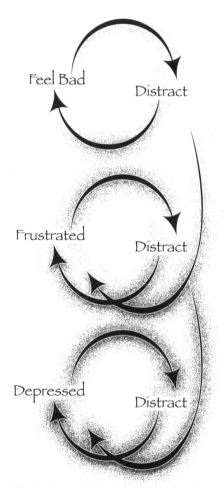

Figure 5: The Feel Bad/Distract/Frustrated/Depressed Cycle

the problem. The Tertiary Feeling of depression is a safety valve. It moves in to save you from self-destruction, not to cause it, as many believe. It says, "If you keep this up, you're going to explode. It's time to take a break and recharge. You need to rest. Go to bed. Take it easy for a while."

While you're experiencing this Tertiary Feeling, your drive to satisfy the need is depressed for a while. After you've rested up, it returns. You begin moving back up from feeling depressed to risking frustration again, by attempting once more to satisfy the need, want or desire. As you make this move, it's important to remember that *the message of frustration is that you must do something different from what you were doing before. Otherwise, you'll again become frustrated and again fall back into depression.*

Figure 5 illustrates this cycle of feeling bad, then distracting and experiencing frustration, which leads to depression.

We're always risking frustration. However, if we abandon the behaviors we know from experience aren't effective, we greatly decrease the possibility of frustration. At the same time, we increase the probability of success in satisfying the feeling.

For example, the individual who eats out of loneliness will surely become frustrated, because nothing she can eat will fulfill her need for a relationship. If she continues this behavior, it will lead to frustration and eventually depression. However, if she steps back and sees the connection between her eating and loneliness, she can start taking actions that will actually fulfill the need of having relationships.

This takes courage. It requires facing the reality of our lives—what we're missing out on, how we've failed ourselves and whether we are taking responsibility for satisfying our own needs. It requires the willingness to experience our feelings while we look for a response that will be truly satisfying to us. And to recognize that the response that will meet our need may not be a response we feel comfortable making.

Chapter 5

The 1-2-3 Self-Coaching Process

When we're learning about our feelings, it's important to recognize that we experience basically just two states of emotion. *We're either in the state of having satisfied a present need, which we experience as emotionally pleasurable, or we're in the state of being unsatisfied, which is emotionally painful.*

These two states are at opposite ends of a continuum. We're always moving from one to the other, which means we're always in varying degrees of satisfaction or dissatisfaction. The vocabulary of the secret language of feelings names the emotions we experience when we're dissatisfied.

Fortunately, this vocabulary is relatively small. We'll generally be focusing on only ten words and their meanings. The first eight words on the list are Primary Feelings. Any one of these Primary Feelings could replace the word "Bad" in the "Feeling Bad" cycle shown in the illustrations from the previous chapter.

The Secret Language of Feelings

The Primary Feelings are:
   1. Boredom
   2. Anger
   3. Guilt
   4. Sadness
   5. Loneliness
   6. Inadequacy
   7. Stress
   8. Fear

The 2 other feelings we work with are:
   9. The Secondary Feeling of Frustration
   10. The Tertiary Feeling of Depression

The first eight feelings, our Primary Feelings, are the ones that most trouble us, leading us into a life of distraction and unhealthy stress.

There are many more words in the English vocabulary that describe feelings, but they aren't used here for a variety of reasons. Some of those alternative names for feelings are euphemisms for the Primary Feelings; they are socially acceptable expressions of unpleasant or negative emotions.

Other missing words express a particular level of intensity of a feeling already on the list. For example, levels of anger include being irritated, upset, pissed-off, furious and enraged. Levels of fear include being concerned, anxious, nervous, worried, frightened and scared to death. As you can see, each of these words expresses a particular flavor or intensity of the Primary Feeling, from mild to extreme.

Finally, there are many words that aren't useful for our purposes, because they don't give us enough information. For example, when you say you feel bad, hurt or out of sorts, it's almost meaningless. It only describes that you're in a state of emotional discomfort or pain, but it doesn't indicate anything about the nature of the discomfort, which would tell us about the need that's unsatisfied.

Using one of these indefinite words is like saying that one of the lights on the dashboard of the car is lit up. That information is useless, unless we know the name of the light and the car's need it's related to. ***Only when we accurately describe what we're feeling can we make the appropriate response.*** In the same vein, when we learn to name our feelings and understand the message they have for us, we can identify the action that will satisfy the unmet need.

Feelings and Associated Needs

Each of the ten feeling words in our vocabulary list is associated with a need, want or desire, as shown below:

Emotional Pain	*Need, Want, Desire*
1. Boredom	To grow through challenge
2. Anger	To experience fairness *for* self and others
3. Guilt	To be fair *to* others
4. Sadness	To keep valued things and people
5. Loneliness	To have meaningful relationships

6. Inadequacy   To feel good enough/adequate
7. Stress   To have success in managing one's life
8. Fear   To feel safe
9. Frustration   To meet needs through own efforts
10. Depression   To be effective and hopeful

In addition to the ten feelings listed above, there's also a chapter on sympathy. This is because sympathy can cause us to feel "bad" when someone else is hurting. It can also activate feelings from our past through emotional resonance. Until we can separate our feelings from the past from the feelings/needs of the other, it's difficult to recognize what response—if any—is appropriate.

If you're like most of the clients we see at the Banyan Hypnosis Center for Training and Services, you probably have never been aware of this direct correlation between feelings and needs. If so, you might be feeling more hopeful right now, because you have information that can change your life. In the next section, you'll learn how to put this information to use.

The 1-2-3 of The Secret Language

Knowledge isn't power, it's potential. Implementation is power. As you learn the secret language of feelings, you also need to learn how to implement it. It's only through the implementation of this information that you can take back your power, gaining control over how you feel and what you do.

The key to implementing the secret language of feelings is

The 1-2-3 Self-Coaching Process

using this three-stage process:

1. Identify/name the feeling.

**2. Identify the cause of the feeling
(unfilled need, want or desire).**

**3. Identify a satisfying response—that is, an action
that fulfills the need, want or desire.**

It's that simple—but it may not be easy! As you learn the language, you'll undoubtedly learn a great deal about yourself. That can be a somewhat challenging process, especially if you've been cut off from your feelings for a long time. Some of us, even upon self-examination, still have no idea how we feel, other than that we feel "good" or "bad." For those of us who experience such difficulty, it's likely that our feelings have been off limits for so long that we've become deaf to the voice inside of us. But with some determination and perhaps guidance, we can reclaim this important ability—the ability to be aware of our internal sense of what we need and what we need to do.

Now that we know the process, let's see how it works!

Step One: Naming The Feeling

Naming the feeling is extremely important to the **1-2-3** process. If we can name the feeling, we can identify the cause of the feeling. So how do we go from just knowing we feel bad to identifying a specific Primary Feeling?

The Secret Language of Feelings

This is easier for some people than it is for others. From my experience, women in general are able to identify their feelings more easily than men. (Men, on the other hand, identify the cause more easily.) Both men and women who routinely ignore their feelings, or who repress and suppress them, will find identifying the Primary Feeling to be a challenge. But the benefits of knowing the secret language of feelings can't be realized unless they can take this first step.

If you're out of touch with what you're feeling, you'll benefit in many ways from becoming more aware of this inner voice. Take time to sit somewhere quiet, with no distractions. Pay attention to what you're feeling and where you're feeling it. Listen to any insights that come to you. You might benefit from doing some journaling. Once you begin to pay attention to your inner life, you'll get better and better at identifying your feelings.

Sometimes, you may be stuck at trying to identify the Primary Feeling. In that case, you might find it useful to skip to Step Two, Identifying the Cause. In the same way that knowing the feeling can point to the cause or need, knowing the unfilled need (cause) can also point to the associated feeling. To illustrate, we'll once again return to the example of the car with the dashboard lights.

Imagine you're in a foreign land. You're driving a foreign car, which has all its lights and gauges labeled in a language that you don't understand. Suddenly, one of the lights on the dashboard starts flashing. You're out in the countryside and there's no one to help you. What would you do? Would you just keep going, hoping for the best, but in a constant state of stress that grows stronger by the mile? Or would you do a little guesswork and investigate?

Let's say you decide to do a little investigating. As you look at the flashing light on the dashboard, you think, "I have a light just like that on the dashboard of my car back home. When it lights up, the oil's always been low." Now you have a hypothesis, an educated guess that you can test.

You pull over and check the oil level, which you find is quite low. This is evidence that your hypothesis is right, and you begin to feel more confident that you can solve the problem. All you have to do is get to the next town where there's a service station. When you get there, you add oil to the reservoir. Voila! The light goes out. You've identified the cause of the light going on (low oil reserves), so you now know the name of the light (oil).

You can use a similar process to learn about your feelings and the associated needs, wants and desires. If you're feeling bad but you can't name the feeling more specifically, guess! Then see if it makes sense by looking at what's going on in your life. **When you identify the cause of the feeling, you'll know the name of the feeling.** Below are some examples showing how the state of your life (cause) indicates the Primary Feeling you're experiencing.

Have you lost your job, house, or savings? You may be feeling sad.

Is someone treating you unfairly? You're probably feeling angry.

Do you feel you've treated someone else unfairly? You may be feeling guilty.

Have you been spending time alone instead of building significant relationships? You may be lonely.

Are you feeling life is repetitive with no challenges? You may be feeling bored.

Did you grow up in a family where you were constantly criticized? You may feel inadequate.

Do you have too much to do and not enough time or resources? You may be feeling stressed.

Have you failed in your attempts to satisfy any of the above? You may be feeling frustrated.

Are you beginning to think about giving up? You may be starting to feel depressed.

Learning this language requires that you become accustomed to observing yourself to see how well you're meeting your needs. If you're not sure how you feel, guess! Once you have a hypothesis, look at your life and see if it makes sense. Then begin to fulfill the need. If you guessed right, then the feeling should go away. The feeling will not return until you find yourself in a state where you're again not satisfying the need.

Step Two: Identify the Cause

Much has already been discussed in the previous section about how to determine the cause of the feeling, but let me go into more detail. When you name the feeling, you begin an investigation into how you came to feel this way. Looking back at our list (pg. 50), you learn that sadness comes from loss. Anger comes from the perception of unfairness. Loneliness comes from not having satisfying relationships, and so on.

To really make this step useful, however, you'll need to go further than these kinds of generalities. If you're sad, you need to not only acknowledge the loss, but to identify what or who exactly was lost. If you're lonely, you need to identify which relationships are missing from your life. Do you have a spouse? Are your friendship needs being met? Are you used to having a favorite pet around and now you're separated? Loneliness can be very specific. If you're lonely for your wife or husband, you can be in the company of others, such as your mother, sister or brother, and still feel very lonely.

The more specific you're when determining the cause, the more successful you're likely to be at deciding on a satisfying response. By a satisfying response, I mean the action you need to take in order to satisfy the need, want or desire.

Step Three: Identify a Satisfying Response

If you're one of those people who has a hard time identifying feelings, you may also find it somewhat challenging to come up with a satisfying response—an action that satisfies the need, want or desire. This is because when you ignore your feelings, you're also ignoring your needs.

However, satisfying the cause of the feeling eliminates the cause, or at least reduces it. For example, if you feel stressed, the feeling indicates that you have too much to do and not enough time or resources to do it well. Some satisfying responses might be to reduce the number of obligations you have, to prioritize or to get help.

In the next part of the book, I'll show you how you can use this secret language for each of the ten major feelings. I'll also suggest satisfying responses for each of the feelings. Although the list may be useful as an example, it's important for you to come up with your own list for each of the feelings. Your list will more accurately reflect who you are and what responses would be satisfying to you. Get a notebook now, so you'll have it ready when you begin work on Part Two.

Of course, the idea is that you'll take the actions you list under Step 3: Identify a Satisfying Response. ***Doing 1-2-3 without taking action is using the process as a distractor.*** It may make you feel better for a while, but it won't satisfy your unfilled needs.

Even when you do start taking your listed actions, you may find that they aren't as satisfying as you thought they would be. If that's the case, remember that doing the unsatisfying action over and over again, or faster and harder, probably won't make it successful—it will only set you up for frustration, and you now know where that leads. What's needed is a new approach. You'll have to ask yourself, "How else can I satisfy this need?"

Start Using 1-2-3 Now!

It would be best if you start learning the secret language of feelings before you begin to experience the inevitable pain of life. This makes a great deal of sense when you think about it. If you wanted to be able to speak Spanish for an upcoming vacation to Spain or Mexico, for example, you would begin studying the language long before your trip.

Take a moment now to remember times when you felt bad. What were you feeling? How could you have responded in a more satisfying way? If you give it some thought, you can quickly come up with the feelings have caused you problems in the past. With further thought, you can also come up with some pretty good hypotheses as to what has caused you to feel this way. You might even have some ideas about doable actions that would satisfy your unmet needs. It's also a good idea to enlist the help of family and friends in the process.

Part Two of this book gives you the opportunity to begin the process. It not only addresses each of the ten feelings in depth, but also includes a worksheet for each with space for you to write your insights and list some satisfying responses that call to you. Buy your notebook and make a commitment now that you'll write down some ideas as soon as you finish reading each chapter. If you wait until you're mad, sad or otherwise feeling "bad," the last thing you'll want to do is look at the worksheets. But if you've already made entries in your notebook, it will become an effective tool for creating a more satisfying life.

Your emotions are like an internal compass. When you can read it, understand it and use it, you will be able to move your life in the direction you want to go.

Part Two:

Self-Coaching
for a Satisfying Life

Introduction to Part Two

In Part One of "The Secret Language of Feelings," you were introduced to a whole new model for thinking about and reacting to your feelings. In Part Two, you'll learn how this model applies to each of the Primary Feelings and have a chance to practice **1-2-3 Self-Coaching** with them.

1-2-3 Self-Coaching is designed to be an effective tool for self-discovery and self-care. The more you use it, the easier it will become to identify your feelings. You'll probably notice that you have a particular "feeling vocabulary, " a constellation of feelings that occur together. For instance, some people might often feel inadequate, guilty and sad, but rarely feel angry. You'll also become clear about what your needs are and the kind of responses that are satisfying.

To get the most out of this book, I suggest you buy a notebook to use when doing the worksheets at the end of chapters 6-16. Those of you do so—and who adopt **1-2-3** as an ongoing practice—will soon recognize it as a powerful guide for creating a life full of satisfaction and joy.

The most deceptive and misunderstood feeling is boredom. Don't be fooled— it is often other feelings in disguise.

Chapter 6

The Wisdom of Feeling Bored

When you feel bored, it is a voice inside of you saying, "I need to experience growth and challenge in my life."

You may be wondering why Feeling Bored is the first Primary Feeling on my list. After all, the list includes so many really unpleasant emotions, like Feeling Angry or Feeling Sad. In my practice, I find that clients will quickly label the uncomfortable feeling that they are experiencing as being bored. But often this label just doesn't add up. If your life is full of challenge, you're not bored! However, many of my clients insist that boredom is the only feeling that they can come up with, at least at first.

This may be because boredom is the one feeling that we don't feel bad about admitting to. Usually when we admit something, we fear others will judge us negatively. We wouldn't want people to know that we feel lonely, angry, guilty or insecure, for example, because they would make judgments about our value and worthiness or criticize us.

In contrast, we don't perceive being bored in such negative ways. On the contrary, we might actually think of it as an indication that we are superior. We're bored because we're smarter and more energetic than those around us. Because we're handling everything so well, life isn't much of a challenge.

People are all too quick to mistakenly come to the conclusion that they are bored for another reason. When they feel fidgety or generally uncomfortable, they find those feelings of discomfort are alleviated when they keep themselves busy. On the surface, this conclusion seems to make sense. However, if you find that you're driven to constantly stay busy with work or other activities such as cleaning house, it may mean that you're just distracting yourself from some other feeling that would cause you pain if you slowed down a little. Some other need, want or desire is not being met. Distraction is a coping strategy, but it does not go to the root of the problem.

When it comes to whether or not you're satisfying your needs, wants, and desires, there is no difference between you distracting yourself with odd jobs around the house and the alcoholic who distracts with a drink in order to cope with feeling bad. It's still a rut of distraction, and that rut leads to further pain and even addiction.

Have you ever heard the saying, "When life gives you

lemons, make lemonade?" Please don't do that. If you don't want or like lemons, get rid of them! You see, the lemons represent unpleasant emotions, such as a sour mood. Making lemonade is the equivalent of adding something sweet to the sour. You are much better off if you get rid of the sour mood or whatever is causing it.

For example, if you're lonely and you mislabel it as being bored, instead of building new relationships, you will just busy yourself with something else you enjoy, such as eating ice cream. The loneliness you feel is like the lemons. The ice cream is the sweetness added to the lemons to make them into lemonade. The problem is that when you get done with the ice cream, you will begin to feel bad again, and again you will crave the ice cream (or whatever your favorite distractor may be.)

Bill's Story

Bill's case is a good example of needing to find something to do that was challenging in a positive way.

Bill was a young man in his mid-20s who came to me for hypnotherapy because he wanted to lose 15 pounds. I introduced him to the secret language of feelings and began the hypnotherapy process with some hypnotic suggestions to help him change his eating habits. The suggestions focused on helping him accomplish two things. First, whenever he felt the urge to eat, he was to check to see if he really was physically hungry. Second, if he wasn't physically hungry, he was to do the **1-2-3** of the secret language.

After doing **1-2-3** for a week, Bill came back for his second session. As we talked, we learned that Bill was chronically bored. He was bored at work, bored at home and bored with his relationship. I call this a theme, by which I mean that there was one predominant need in his life that was not being met, in this case, the need for challenges and growth.

When Bill and I went over the work he had done with **1-2-3**, we found out that there were only two things he liked to do when he was bored: watch television and eat.   As a result, he had developed the habit of eating and watching television every evening, a common theme for people who live alone.

We worked together to come up with a list of other things Bill might find both interesting and challenging. One possibility Bill identified was taking guitar lessons. He also decided to check into taking some business classes because he thought he might like to go into business for himself some day.

Bill came back into my office the following week looking energized and excited. He announced that he had lost 3 pounds during the last week. I asked him if he had gone on a diet, and he said, "No, I got a life!"

Bill explained that when he started looking into the guitar lessons, he realized he wasn't all that interested in them. However, when he started looking into class offerings at business schools and colleges, he became very excited about the possibilities.   He learned a lot about himself during that time, the urge to snack dwindled down to nothing and he gained a great deal of control over his eating habits.

Now it's your turn to learn more about this often misused and mislabeled feeling. Do you often feel bored? Does it make sense, given your life? Is your life challenging enough for you? Interesting enough? Remember, being busy doesn't mean that you're sufficiently challenged. If you only do the same things over and over again, you can be very busy and bored out of your mind!

The challenges that you need to have in your life are the kinds of challenges that cause you to grow as an individual, the activities that you find to be a learning experience. These are satisfying activities—and they're often also fun and even exciting.

Doing 1-2-3 with "Feeling Bored"

1. Identify/name the feeling: Bored or another name for bored that expresses a particular level of intensity such as lethargic, antsy, etc.

2. Identify the cause of the feeling: Not being challenged in some area of your life.

"Not being challenged" is a general way to express the cause of feeling bored. How you experience this lack of challenge, as well as how it can be satisfied, is highly individual. It's important for you to take time to explore what is happening—and not happening—in your life.

Be really specific. Instead of saying "I'm bored. Nothing

interests me," you might say "My kids are in school now and they don't need me as much. I don't know what to do with my time, now that I'm not so busy raising them." This kind of information gives you much more to work with and points the way for further exploration.

3. Identify a satisfying response. Remember that a satisfying response satisfies the need, want or desire. In this case it needs to be an activity that will be a growth experience. Such activities are usually fun and interesting.

The following is just a list of suggested activities. The one you come up with will be different, because it will include the particular activities that you find fun or interesting, or have identified as areas where you want or need growth. Just use this list to get started. Here's a suggestion. When you write your list, use "a, b, c," etc. to avoid confusion with **1-2-3**.

> a. Do something new and different or something you have always wanted to do.
>
> b. Buy a computer and learn how to use it.
>
> c. Become an expert on topic you're interested in.
>
> d. Get a new pet and learn all about it.
>
> e. Learn how to train your dog or cat. (Lots of luck with the cat!)
>
> f. Pursue a new hobby such as photography or woodworking.
>
> g. Organize your photos into albums or research family history.
>
> h. Buy some seeds and plant a flower or vegetable garden.
>
> i. Get involved in a good cause or community service.

The Wisdom of Feeling Bored

j. Take a class—just for fun or to further a job change you've been thinking about.

k. Learn to play chess or a card game such as bridge.

l. Learn a foreign language—then take a trip to the country where it's spoken.

m. Plan a theme trip, such as visiting historical sites in the East.

n. Take up bird watching and join your local bird-watching club.

o. Teach an adult education class on a topic that interests you.

p. Learn yoga or some other kind of stretching or relaxation technique.

q. Start or join a book club.

r. Plan a family reunion.

s. Call all the people you haven't talked to for awhile.

t. Learn how to make home repairs—then make some!

u. Start training now to run a marathon.

v. Ask a kid or senior to tell you a story and write it down.

w. Learn about the kind of antiques or collectibles you like and look for a find at garage sales and flea markets.

x. Learn how your car or motorcycle works.

y. Learn to play a musical instrument.

z. Do anything that I didn't list here—as long as it isn't illegal, immoral or fattening!

Bonus 1-2-3: The Need to Exercise

This is an interesting variation on the feeling of being bored. Our parents or grandparents probably worked very hard just to meet their basic needs for food and shelter. Their didn't have to worry about getting exercise, because their lives were full of physical exertion such as scrubbing floors, chopping wood, walking in order to visit neighbors or to go to work, etc.

We live in a world where much of what we do each day can be accomplished by simply pushing a button. As a result, many of us have to schedule visits to the health club or sessions on our home exercise equipment in order to satisfy our need for physical exertion. And when life gets hectic, exercise is the thing that drops by the wayside.

When you aren't getting the exercise you need, you may experience it as the feeling of being bored. Or you may feel so fidgety that you can't sit still. Could it be that your unconscious mind is trying to send you a signal that says, "I feel like I need to get some exercise"? Could there be a clearer way for this secret language to tell you that you need to put more motion into your life than sending you a signal that makes you feel antsy, as if you can't sit still?

Next time that happens to you, do this **1-2-3**.

1. Identify/name the feeling: Antsy, or a name that expresses a particular level of intensity such as, can't sit still, bouncing off the wall. Not to be confused with feeling nervous, which is fear.

2. Identify the cause of the feeling: You haven't been getting enough exercise

3. Identify a satisfying response. This can be any activity involving physical exercise that you like. Start to:

a. Walk, run or swim.

b. Go biking, in-line skating or skiing.

c. Do Jazzercize or aerobics.

d. Go dancing, hiking or rock climbing.

e. Get up and move!

The satisfying response is to get moving, but in order to make sure you exercise regularly—thus avoiding the antsy feeling—you need to you set up a regular program. In other words, plan for time to meet your need to exercise.

Because of the busy lives we lead, we need to plan time to take care of our needs. Time to be with our friends and family so that we don't become lonely. Time for growth so we don't become bored. We're better off and lead happier lives if we are proactive in fulfilling our needs, wants and desires.

1-2-3 Worksheet: Bored

In your **1-2-3** notebook, write down your responses to the following steps. The more specific you can be, the more useful your notebook will be in helping you create a satisfying life, both now and in the future.

Step 1. Identify the feeling. Bored or another name for bored that expresses a particular level of intensity such as lethargic, antsy, etc.

Step 2. Identify the cause. Feeling unchallenged. Be specific about how feeling challenged shows up in your life.

Step 3. List some satisfying responses. Write down ways to make life more challenging in a positive way, such as learning something new or doing something fun and exciting. Remember that it may take some time to find the response that really is the most satisfying. Add resources and people who will help you satisfy this need.

Chapter 7

The Wisdom of Feeling Angry

Anger is a voice inside that says, "I think what is going on here is unfair!"

I often surprise my clients by telling them that anger is my favorite feeling! This is usually quite startling, because anger is one of the most taboo of all feelings. You can count on it: If you become angry and you dare show even a hint of it, people will judge you negatively. They will think that you're bad or dangerous. No wonder anger is one of the most misunderstood and most suppressed of all emotions.

Some time ago I was talking to a friend who is a social worker with about 20 years of experience working with individuals in emotional pain. When I shared with him my idea that all feelings are good, he shook his head and said, "Sorry, Cal, I can't buy it. What about anger? People do such terrible things when they become angry."

"That's not anger's fault," I replied. "Anger is good. It's your honest reaction to your perceptions. It's what you do with that anger that's either good, bad or ineffective."

I don't think I convinced my friend. When we ended our conversation, he still had a somewhat skeptical view of my odd ideas. It is, in part, for him and other helping professionals that I am writing this book.

How Anger Can be Good

As we discuss the feeling of anger and all its variations, I want to stress that *all of our emotions come from our perceptions*. The perceptions leading to the feeling of anger come from two very different perspectives.

The first perspective is that of our long-standing beliefs about what's "right" and "wrong" and how things "should" be. If we perceive that people or a situation are as they should be, then we feel they (or life in general) are fair. They meet our expectations. If not, we perceive them as being unfair, which generates anger.

The other perspective is directly related to our current mood. Say we've been working very hard for a specific result and things aren't turning out as planned. We're tired and frustrated. Nothing in the project is working. Not only that, we start thinking nothing in our life is working, either. The thought that comes to mind is, "It's not fair!" or "It's not right!," especially given our efforts and good intentions.

The Wisdom of Feeling Angry

So anger reveals to us our own sense of fairness and of right and wrong. *When we perceive a circumstance as being unfair to ourselves or the people and things that we care about, we feel angry.* Our anger motivates us to do something about it. When the energy behind anger is misdirected, we may have a tantrum or do something equally ineffective—or we may do something that's actually harmful to ourselves and others. *When the energy behind anger is directed in a positive way, we actively seek out ways to create fairness.* Many programs that protect and serve the young and/or helpless in our society were prompted by anger at an unfair situation and the need for social justice.

Anger can also reveal to us the rigidity of our thinking. If we have very fixed ideas about how people should act, we become angry when they do something contrary to our ideas. This kind of anger can lead to estrangement between parents and children, between siblings, between colleagues. We all know someone who hasn't spoken to a parent or sibling for years because an offended sense of right and wrong has become a barrier to communication.

Finally—and perhaps most importantly—anger reveals to us our fears. In fact, all of our uncomfortable or painful emotions arise from fear (See Chapter 13). *Whenever we experience anger, we're experiencing fear that the situation we have perceived to be unfair might also be harmful.* Thus, anger can be best understood as an alarm saying "Look out, this is unfair! And this unfairness may hurt me or someone or something that I care about."

We can think of anger as a biofeedback system. When it's

activated by expectations, beliefs and perhaps our current mood, it shouts, "Be afraid! Be concerned! This is not fair! Take action!" Its purpose is to push us into taking action, into seeking fairness. We can only feel safe and secure when we're being treated fairly and can reasonably expect to be treated fairly in the future.

Once again, I want to emphasize that anger comes from our perceptions. *Since anger comes from perceptions, it's absolutely critical to do a reality check when doing 1-2-3 with this emotion.* Ask yourself these questions: Is the situation really unfair? Am I over-reacting because of emotional resonance? Or am I so tired that everything seems unfair?

When we're faced with an illness or setback of some kind, we often think, "Why me?" Or we say, "That's not fair, I didn't do anything to deserve that." But if we can look past our situation, we can see that it's just life. Illness and accidents happen to everyone, so in a way, it is fair. *If we can find even some degree of fairness in the situation, the pressure of anger is immediately reduced or even eliminated altogether.*

My Story

I like to use my own experience to illustrate how finding fairness in a situation can change perception. I once had a terrible pattern of becoming angry and aggressive when driving, even to the point of being a danger when behind the wheel. When my anger scared my family one day, I realized I had to change. I decided to put what I was learning about the secret language of feelings to

The Wisdom of Feeling Angry

good use. I suppose this is why anger is one of my favorite feelings—it's taught me a great deal about myself and my perceptions and beliefs.

As I focused on the idea that all feelings are good and that anger comes from the perception of unfairness, I realized I was angry because of my own misconception. My whole perspective about other drivers on the road was incorrect and based in fear! Somewhere in my subconscious mind I believed that what motivated the other drivers' actions was aggression toward me or dangerous carelessness that put me at risk. I thought that it was my responsibility to teach them a lesson—if I was aggressive toward them, they would learn they couldn't mess with me and get away with it! And that made me feel safer.

Then it dawned on me. All the things those other drivers had been doing that threw me into a rage—going too fast or too slow, or pulling out without looking or drifting into my lane of traffic— were things I had done myself! And since I had done each of the things that made me mad, in a way it was fair.

The question now was, why did I become so angry, even enraged, when others did what I had been doing? That was easily explained by the principle of emotional resonance. I had been carrying so much anger from my past, that when I became angry while driving, all of the old anger cascaded down into the present. Anger based in the situation of the moment combined with anger resonating from my past, turning what was an irritating situation into a very dangerous situation. My anger motivated me to "show them," which resulted in the uncalled-for behavior that we call road rage.

I was committed to changing my behavior. I realized I needed a way to instantly switch my perception from the old way of thinking to a new, enlightened way of thinking and acting. I decided that if someone ever did one of those things I used to get enraged about, I would simply say to myself, "I've done that."

It didn't take very long to have a chance to put this to a test. I was on my way to work a day or two later, driving my big red four-wheel drive pickup truck. I came to a main street where I had to make a right turn. I wound up just sitting there as the traffic went by, each oncoming vehicle evenly spaced out just far enough apart that I couldn't make my move out onto the highway. I was starting to get a little impatient, thinking to myself, "I can't believe this!"

This reaction could be understood as anger, because it just didn't seem fair that this should be happening while I was on my way to work. And it was certainly taking much longer than usual to make this turn. Suddenly, I could see that there was a break in the traffic such that the cars were going to be spaced far enough apart for me to be able to make my turn.

Just as that space approached the intersection and I was ready to really "step on it" and make the turn, a little sports car, whose driver had gotten sick and tired of waiting for that big truck in front of him to make its move, zoomed out from behind me, pulled in front of me and turned right, blocking me from taking advantage of

The Wisdom of Feeling Angry

the break in traffic I had been waiting for. Then I felt it! The old pattern hit me like a kick to the chest, and the adrenaline flushed into my system. I was fighting mad!

But I had made a promise to change, so I started repeating "I've done that." I repeated it over and over like a mantra until I began to take back control and the desire for retribution began to fade. The feeling of anger didn't instantly disappear, but I could feel a definite difference.

Remember that anger is based in fear. The perception of danger had released a dose of adrenaline into my system, and I felt my nerves and muscles twitch and tighten in response to the "fight or flight" response. But rather than feeding the fear, I continued to repeat the statement, "That's okay, I've done that." This statement reminded me that the situation was not threatening and that it was—in a sort of cosmic way—fair.

I felt great. I had won. Not a battle with the man in the little red sports car, but a battle with an old problem. When I said to myself, "I've done that too!" it was a great release, a personal triumph. I felt like a changed man—and I was a changed man.

I began to use this understanding with everyone in my life. Indeed, if I was really honest with myself about most of the things other people did that made me angry, I had to admit I had done something similar at one time or another. So I could say to myself, "That's okay, I've done that too," and almost instantly regain my composure and be more patient. If I hadn't done the exact thing that the other person did, I would try to think of a circumstance where I might have. This exercise resulted in a much greater understanding of others, as well as a greater capacity for compassion. I started feeling really proud of myself, and all of my relationships began to improve.

Using this process, I was able to greatly reduce or eliminate the anger caused in the present. But you may wonder how I got rid of all the pent-up anger which came from my past. *A major step was realizing that all of my anger came from my perceptions, both past and present.* I worked on changing my perceptions about the past, both consciously and subconsciously, through hypnotic and spiritual practices such as 7th Path™ Self-Hypnosis. I learned that to really become free of the anger I was carrying around inside of me, I had to forgive those I believed had treated me unfairly in the past.

Doing 1-2-3 with "Feeling Angry"

1. Identify/name the feeling: Angry or another name that expresses a particular level of intensity such as irritated, ticked, hurt, mad, enraged, etc.

2. Identify the cause of the feeling: The cause of anger is the perception that something is unfair to you or to someone or something you care about—and it may possibly be hurtful to you or others important to you. The specific perception or event is highly individual.

3. Identify a satisfying response: Below is a short outline of the steps you can take to determine what kind of response to feeling angry will be satisfying.

    A. Do a reality check. Is your perception of the situation accurate? Is it really unfair?

    B. If the situation is unfair, attempt to make it fair— that's what anger is for.

    C. If the situation can't be made fair, forgive.

As you'll see, we often begin doing **1-2-3** with a reality check. In this case, doing a reality check to determine if the situation really is unfair might change your perception, allowing you to see it more fairly. The process of challenging your perception is more easily done when you've cooled down enough to think clearly about the event that generated the anger. Once you have, you can ask yourself, "Is what happened really unfair?"

To help you answer that question, it's a good idea to get another person's view of the situation. You might even decide there's value in listening to the other side with a more open mind. You can then step back and look at the big picture from a different perspective.

From this new perspective, you might discover that you were reacting out of being frustrated, tired or oversensitive. You might discover that the situation had an element of fairness. Or, you might recognize that while the situation was unfair, it was equally unfair to everyone, making it fair in kind of a tangential way. If any of the above is true to your circumstances, your perspective will change and your anger will be reduced or eliminated.

If, however, the situation really is unfair—as in the case of harassment, for example—your anger can be recognized as a strong motivation to make it fair or more fair. This is what the feeling of anger is for. If your anger is "righteous anger," you might list one or more of the following steps under Identify a Satisfying Response: Let others know that the situation is unfair. Communicate to the person who can take action to change it. Contact a group that stands up for right, so you have a chance to even out the power difference. You might even turn to the legal profession if that's appropriate for the situation.

The Benefits of Forgiveness

Sometimes there isn't anything you can do about what has happened—the event is long past, for example, or there are no actions that will make the situation more fair. If that's the case and you're still experiencing emotional pain, forgiving those involved is the only way you can move forward with your life. Real forgiveness reduces the anger and frees you from the past.

Many people don't understand what it means to forgive, so they feel they will lose something if they do. But it's possible to forgive in a very adult and intelligent way. I'd like to share some pointers on how to forgive almost anyone, set yourself free from the past and really heal.

The Wisdom of Feeling Angry

First of all, it's important to recognize that forgiveness doesn't necessarily benefit the person you forgive. It doesn't mean that you like the person or what he or she did. It doesn't require that you tell the person you have forgiven him or her. Nor does it require that you forget what has happened, thereby opening yourself up to a repeat of the hurtful behavior.

You're the one who gets the benefit from forgiveness, because you've set yourself free. Forgiveness gives you back your mental and emotional energy, allowing you to focus on the pleasurable and productive things of life. Forgiveness gives you peace of mind when all other things fail to.

Realize that until you forgive the one who hurt you, he or she is still hurting you, perhaps long after she has stopped thinking about you and the situation. Forgiveness is a way to stop that other person from hurting you and the other people in your life who care about you. Forgiveness can be made easier by trying to understand contributing factors regarding what happened. It can be easier if you can see how the actions also hurt the person who hurt you. The process of forgiveness can also be encouraged by working with someone trained in using the secret language of feelings to help others, such as a properly trained hypnotherapist, counselor or psychologist.

1-2-3 Worksheet: Angry

In your **1-2-3** notebook, write down your responses to the following steps. The more specific you can be, the more useful your notebook will be in helping you create a satisfying life, both now and in the future.

Step 1. Identify the Feeling. Angry or another name for angry that expresses a particular level of intensity such as irritated, ticked, hurt, mad, enraged, etc.

Step 2. Identify the Cause. Something has happened that you perceive as being unfair. Describe the unfair situation.

Step 3. List some satisfying responses. In order to help you identify what responses will be truly satisfying, follow the outline below.

A. Do a reality check. Is the situation really unfair? If not, how can you change your perception?

B. If it's really unfair, how can you make it fair or more fair?

C. If it is unfair and there's no way of making it more fair, who can you forgive?

Chapter 8

The Wisdom of Feeling Guilty

Anger has a twin sister and her name is Guilt. When you feel guilty it is a voice inside of you saying, "I feel I've been unfair to someone."

Guilt and anger are closely related because they're both caused by the perception of unfairness. In the case of anger, the cause was unfairness perceived as being directed at you or someone you care about. *Guilt is caused by the perception of unfairness directed at someone else, caused by you.*

The only difference between anger and guilt is the direction of the unfairness. They're both based in fear. In the case of anger, you're afraid that the unfair situation may harm you or someone that you care about. In the case of guilt, *you're afraid that the unfair thing that you did will either harm someone you care about, or you will be harmed as a result* (i.e., self-judgment, social judgment, spiritual judgment and all of the consequences that result from that judging).

For example, let's say that a friend of yours asks you to help her on a particular day. Then someone else invites you to go shopping on the same day. You can't do both, and going shopping will be a lot more fun. So you convince yourself that your friend really doesn't need your help—she's easily managed similar situations on her own before—and you go shopping instead. Then you feel guilty because you let your friend down.

If you're able to make the situation between you and your friend right again, the feeling of guilt will dissolve. If you're unable to make it up to your friend, your next option is to forgive yourself. Real self-forgiveness also dissolves the feeling of guilt.

The example above is relatively innocuous. Imagine how much more potent guilt and its attendant feelings can be if the cause is something far more serious, such as causing an accident, losing your child's college money, cheating an employer, or not responding when your presence was critical.

If the situation occurred in the past, there may not be a way to regain a sense of fairness with the individuals involved. This often is the case with war veterans who bring home the spoils of war, only to be plagued by guilt as time passes. Many of them find they must make reparations in any way possible in order to feel free to forgive themselves and move on. If there really is no way to make reparations, that's where self-forgiveness comes in.

The feeling of guilt, then, is an emotional discomfort or pain

that motivates you take responsibility for your actions in a way that avoids negative consequences that might result from causing the unfairness.

Doing 1-2-3 with "Feeling Guilty"

1. Identify/name the feeling: Guilty or a guilty by another name that expresses a particular level of intensity such as being to blame, at fault, shameful, wicked, etc.

2. Identify the cause of the feeling: The perception that you've been unfair to someone else (hurt them in some way, such as let them down) and you fear the consequences.

3. Identify a satisfying response: The ways to reduce the feeling of guilt are the same as for anger, only they go in the other direction.

A. Do a reality check. Is what you did really not fair?

B. If it is unfair, attempt to make the situation fair—
   that's what guilt is for.

C. Forgive yourself.

When you do the reality check, strive to be objective about the situation. Is your perception accurate? Was the situation really unfair? If you find this step difficult, you may choose to talk to someone you trust such as a friend or clergyman to help you view the situation from a new perspective.

If you re-examine the situation and can see it as being more fair, that will lessen or eliminate the guilt. If you see the situation as really unfair and you can make it up to the other person, do so. If there is no way you can make it fair, forgive yourself and move on.

If you find it hard to forgive yourself, you aren't alone. Here are some questions you can answer that might help you. Would you like to have done better? If you knew then what you know now, would you do something differently? If the answer is yes, then remember that you didn't know then what you know now—and that makes you forgivable.

1-2-3 Worksheet: Guilty

In your **1-2-3** notebook, write down your responses to the following steps. The more specific you can be, the more useful your notebook will be in helping you create a satisfying life, both now and in the future.

Step 1. Identify the feeling. Guilty or guilty by another name that expresses a particular level of intensity such as being to blame, at fault, shameful, wicked, etc.

Step 2. Identify the cause. The perception that you've done someone wrong or hurt them in some way—and you may be hurt as a result. Be specific about your situation.

Step 3. List some satisfying responses. In order to help you identify what responses will be truly satisfying, follow the outline below. Add resources and people who will help you satisfy this need.

    A. Do a reality check. Was the act or situation really unfair?

    B. If the act was unfair, make it up to the person. Write down how you might do that.

    C. If you can't make it up to the other person, forgive yourself.

Sadness is often confused with depression. Although they do feel very much alike, they are definately not the same.

Chapter 9

The Wisdom of Feeling Sad

Sadness is a voice that says, "I have lost someone or something important to me."

We long to hold onto the people and things that are important to us. These important people and things fulfill our many human needs, wants and desires. When they remain stable and unchanging, we feel safe and secure because our lives are predictable.

When we experience loss, the resulting feeling is sadness. Losing important people and things leads to pain, but the resulting feeling of sadness is good when you understand the language of emotions.

Sadness is there to tell us that the loss was significant, and that we must now take action to 1) get back who or what was lost, or 2) replace the loss of the important person or thing.

Mary's Story

Some time ago, a client I'll call Mary came into my office. Mary had been diagnosed as being depressed and had been on a variety of medications to treat it. As we began to talk I could see that she felt very sad and was on the verge of tears. Knowing the meaning of sadness, I asked "Who or what did you lose?"

Mary looked shocked, as if I'd I somehow read her heart and spoken to her soul. There was nothing supernatural about what I did—I just used my knowledge of the secret language of feelings. You'll also be able to read others much more accurately as you begin to use what you're learning.

With tears streaming down her face, Mary told me that her mother had died more than two years ago. Try as she might, she was plagued by constant thoughts of her loss.

As Mary described her relationship with her mother, the reason for her chronic and debilitating sadness became apparent. Up to the time of her death, Mary's mother had filled many roles in her daughter's life, thus meeting many of Mary's needs, wants and desires. Because each role her mother filled was very important to Mary, it was difficult for her to recover from the loss.

Mary's mother was her best friend, her confidant and counselor. She was Mary's favorite shopping partner. She was also a loving grandmother to Mary's children and a dependable babysitter. And of course, she had provided all the wonderful nurturing, love and support that are part of a close mother-daughter relationship. In a sense, Mary had not lost just one person when her mother died, but many.

I taught Mary the secret language and gently introduced the idea that when fully understood, the feeling of sadness which she had been experiencing was good in some very specific ways. I explained that once she learned how her sadness was good, she would learn how to do some things that would make her feel better and heal.

From her sessions with me, Mary came to understand that her prolonged sadness over her mother's death was a result of constantly experiencing loss. Every time she needed a friend, she felt sad because she experienced the loss of a friend. Every time she needed a confidant, she felt sad because she had lost the person who filled that role in her life. Every time she wanted to go shopping or do other activities that she enjoyed, she felt sad because the person she had enjoyed doing those activities with was gone. And whenever she needed a babysitter that she could trust with her children, she was saddened because her mother's passing had taken that away also.

Once she understood this, Mary also understood that the sadness was there to motivate her to take the actions necessary to find friends who would fill those roles in her life. She needed to become more social and build new and important relationships so that her life could become full and active again. As she realized there were some actions she could take, she began to feel hopeful and her feelings of depression began to fade. With the support of her family and hypnotherapy, she began to building new relationships.

A New Perspective on Loss

Building new relationships would fill four of the roles Mary's mother had played in her life, reducing Mary's sadness by a great deal. However, the role of mother couldn't be filled by another person. Something else would have to occur in order to lessen the pain Mary felt at the loss of her mother. I knew that unless the way Mary looked at her mother's death changed, she would always feel that loss whenever she thought of her loving mother.

When I asked Mary what she believed happened when someone died, she said she believed in life after death. For her, death was just a passing on to a new life, a spiritual existence.

"It sounds like you don't really believe your mother is gone, never to be seen again," I said. "You fully anticipate being with her again when your time comes, hopefully a long time from now. Is that right?" Mary gave a sigh of relief and began showing signs of hopefulness. Remember, hopefulness is the antidote to depression.

I continued, "So the death of your mother isn't the permanent loss of someone that you love, but rather a temporary separation to be followed by a wonderful, loving reunion. Is that what you're telling me?"

At that thought, Mary immediately began to smile and her

tears stopped flowing. "I haven't really been thinking about it that way," she said.

A light went on inside of Mary as she let the idea of her mother's death be transformed into a temporary separation. Life came back into her eyes and her sadness began melting away. We then began discussing actions she could take to fulfill the needs, wants and desires that had been left unmet since her mother's passing.

"Why didn't anyone ever talk to me this way before?" Mary wondered out loud. "I have been in counseling for so long, and this has helped me more than anything. Before, everything seemed so hopeless. Now I can see that there are some real things that I can do to make myself feel better."

Indeed, as she continued to go through the therapeutic process with me, Mary became more active, which improved her life in many ways. She became a better mother to her own children and a better spouse to her husband.

The steps I went through with Mary in regards to the loss of an important person are also the steps you would go through in regards to the loss of an important object.

First, check your perceptions—has there really been a loss? For example, according to Mary's own beliefs, she had not really "lost" her mother, she was only separated from her. Recognize whether the object can or can't be returned to you or if it needs to be replaced. If it can't be returned, create a plan to replace it.

If it can't be returned or replaced, create a new perspective that lets you come to peace with the loss. Then a natural and healthy process of grief can proceed.

Doing 1-2-3 with "Feeling Sad"

1. Identify/name the feeling: Sad or another name for sadness that expresses a particular level of intensity such as feeling unhappy, down, blue or broken-hearted. Often confused with depression, but not the same.

2. Identify the cause of the feeling: You have lost someone or something that is important to you. Be specific about who or what you have lost and why the loss is significant. Clarify which of your needs, wants or desires the person or item filled.

3. Identify a satisfying response: The kind of actions that will be satisfying in response to sadness depend upon the nature of your loss and the cause of the loss.

    A. Reality check—was there really a loss?

    B. If possible, attempt to get back the person or item lost.

    C. If you can't get the person back, create new relationships that fill your needs.

    D. If you can't get the item back, seek to replace it. If the item is irreplaceable, attempt to fulfill your needs another way.

    E. Allow a healthy process of grieving.

The Wisdom of Feeling Sad

If you have lost someone important to you, see if there's some action you can take to change the situation. For example, if you have lost the association of a spouse, family member, friend or companion through some action that can be made right, do what is necessary to make it right. Then that person might again be part of your life. If you have lost touch with someone important because you haven't taken the time to communicate, make contact.

If your loss has to do with a person of importance to your life, such as a parent or spouse, it's important to recognize that you can't replace an individual the way you might replace a lost item by buying a new one. You may always feel your loss when something triggers a memory, but you can build new relationships that fill your needs. You can find new people to share activities with, to confide in, to rely upon and to love, if you're willing to open yourself up to what life has to offer you.

If you have suffered the loss of a treasured or important item, look for ways to regain what you have lost, if possible. Understand that it might take a while to get the item back. If it can't be recovered, recognize that it can probably be replaced and take steps to do so.

If what you have lost is a precious or valued item that can't be replaced, count your blessings and value what you do have. Although it may seem difficult, consider looking for what advantages might come from the loss. You might find some that are unexpected. For instance, if family papers are destroyed, a positive outcome of the loss might be your heightened awareness of how important family items are and the new ways you devise to keep them safe.

When your loss is real and permanent—when there's no action you can take to change things—allow yourself time to grieve and then begin to move on.

Developing a new perspective is a great help in this process. You might begin the practice of writing down five things you're grateful for each day, at least for awhile. Noticing and expressing gratitude for all the wonderful people and things you still do have around you has a wonderful effect. The more you notice what you have, the richer your life will be. This practice may sound simplistic, but it can make a powerful difference in your life.

1-2-3 Worksheet: Sad

In your **1-2-3** notebook, write down your responses to the following steps. The more specific you can be, the more useful your notebook will be in helping you create a satisfying life, both now and in the future.

Step 1. Identify/name the feeling. Sad or another name for sad that expresses a particular level of intensity such as feeling unhappy, down, blue or broken-hearted.

Step 2. Identify the cause. You have lost an important person or item. Be specific about whom or what you have lost.

Step 3. List some satisfying responses. Use the outline below as a guide. When you have come up with some responses, add resources and people who will support you in meeting your needs.

    A. Do a reality check. Did you really experience a loss?

    B. What can you do to get back the person or item lost?

    C. If you can't get the item back, can you replace it?

    D. If you can't get the person back and you can't replace the item, what actions can you take to fulfill the needs satisfied by the lost person or item?

    E. Recognize when you have done what you can, then allow a healthy process of grieving to occur.

We're designed to be social creatures.
We thrive and grow when we're surrounded
by people we love and care about.

Chapter 10

The Wisdom of Feeling Lonely

When you feel lonely, it's a voice inside of you saying, "I need to be with someone I care about and who cares about me."

In the past few years, I've become aware of something amazing: Most people that I see are living lives of crowded isolation. It seems as though we as individuals, to one extent or another, have lost the ability to build meaningful relationships. Perhaps this is because we're more mobile as a society. Decades ago, most people lived in or not too far from the town they grew up in. As a result, they had a whole lifetime among the same group of people, enjoying the companionship of their extended families and developing relationships. That isn't often the case these days.

Technology may also have contributed to the problem. It's become much easier for us to turn on the television and watch shows about relationships than to actually engage ourselves in them. Or to surf the web and "chat" with faceless "friends" that we'll never meet.

The problem with such activities is that we're genetically designed to gain satisfaction from real relationships. We don't get the same kind of satisfaction from watching television or looking at a glowing computer monitor that we do from looking into the face of someone we really care about. **We're designed to be social creatures; we thrive and grow when we're surrounded by people we love or care about.**

There's no activity, television, food, alcohol, shopping or any other thing that can give us the kind of satisfaction we get from really experiencing being loved by another human being or being part of a group of people who have a common goal or interest.

Sometimes, loneliness can be confused with boredom. You might be thinking, "There's nothing I'm really interested in," when what you are really feeling is, "I wish I had a friend to do something with." Loneliness is also often associated with sadness, although they're quite different. Mary was sad at the death of her mother. She was also lonely, missing human companionship and intimacy. She learned to fill that need by establishing new relationships. The loneliness was good, in that it provided Mary the motivation she needed to learn and use a whole new set of skills for relationship building.

Doing 1-2-3 with "Feeling Lonely"

1. Identify/name the feeling: Lonely or another name that

expresses a particular level of intensity such as left out, isolated, rejected or unwanted. Often confused with bored, but definitely not the same.

2. Identify the cause of the feeling: You are experiencing a good healthy desire for human companionship, because your relationships are lacking.

3. Identify a satisfying response: Make a list of things you can do that will put you in the company of people you care about or people who share you interests. Then do some of them!

Use this list to get your imagination going:

a. Call someone you know and share something meaningful.

b. Plan lunch with friends you haven't seen for awhile.

c. Get a part-time job doing something you enjoy.

d. Join a special-interest club—gardening, bridge, etc.

e. Take dance or music lessons.

f. Volunteer for a good cause.

g. Take a class just to be around others.

h. Become active in your church or find a spiritual community.

i. Meet your neighbors—maybe even have a neighborhood party.

j. Become active politically or in your community.

1-2-3 Worksheet: Lonely

In your **1-2-3** notebook, write down your responses to the following steps. The more specific you can be, the more useful your notebook will be in helping you create a satisfying life, both now and in the future.

Step 1. Identify/name the feeling. Lonely or another name that expresses a particular level of intensity such as left out, isolated, rejected or unwanted.

Step 2. Identify the cause. You aren't experiencing satisfying social relationships. Be specific, for example, do you need a confidant? Someone with whom you can go hiking or traveling? Someone who shares your spiritual beliefs?

Step 3. List some satisfying responses. Follow the outline below as a guide for developing satisfying responses. Add resources and people who will support you in meeting your needs.

> A. Do a reality check. Are you really left out, rejected, and isolated, or do you need a change of perspective?
>
> B. If you need a change of perspective, how can you develop one?
>
> C. If you really are isolated, what can you do to connect with people?
>
> D. What skills can you learn that will help you establish good, healthy relationships?

Chapter 11

The Wisdom of Feeling Inadequate

Inadequacy is a voice inside of you saying, "I feel like there's something wrong with me."

As we were growing up, we all encountered people who decided for one reason or another that there was something wrong with us. They expressed that opinion in both word and deed. Either way, we got the message: You aren't good enough, smart enough, strong enough, etc.

The words spoken can be even more hurtful when they create within us a deep sense of shame, words such as: "You're bad. You've done bad things. I'm ashamed of you! What's the matter with you? Nobody will ever want to be around (or love) someone like you." Such misinformation can have a devastating effect, hurting us emotionally and staying with us long after the event.

On top of that, there were probably situations that caused us to feel and think we were inadequate, unloveable and bad. And even though the negative message may have only been our *perception*, how we imagined others were judging us, it still had a negative effect.

From a hypnotherapist's point of view, children are essentially in hypnosis most of the time, meaning that they are highly suggestible. They remain in this highly suggestible state until they have gathered enough information about the world and matured sufficiently to be able to reject these kinds of negative statements. Remember that children lack the life experiences that allow adults to reject the ideas and opinions of others. As children we often accept incredible things just because the adults around us say that they are true, or act like something is true. Take for example your childhood beliefs in the Easter Bunny, the Tooth Fairy and Santa Claus.

Suggestions that carry a strong negative emotion based in fear may last a great deal longer than the belief in Santa Claus. If a child grows up afraid of the dark because of the "Boogeyman," he or she may reject their belief in the monster as an adult—but still experience being afraid of the dark.

In the same way, **hurtful misinformation about whether we are good enough to be loveable becomes a part of our belief system.** As adults we may consciously reject it, but since our beliefs are held in our subconscious minds, they aren't so easily removed through conscious effort. This is why hypnotherapy can be so effective in helping us rid ourselves of such self-limiting beliefs.

With hypnotherapy, the subconscious mind can receive and use positive suggestions and remove the erroneous beliefs accepted in childhood.

Betty's story

When I conduct training for hypnotherapists, I will often explain how this happens to us by giving this example. Imagine that there's a wonderful little girl named Betty. She is a completely capable 3-year-old. She is completely capable, full of untapped potential waiting to come into full bloom given the right amount of love and encouragement.

One day her father decides to stop off at the toy store on the way home from work. While he is in the store, he decides to buy his darling little girl a ball so that they can play catch together and have some fun. When he gets home, he calls out to Betty who comes running out of her room happy to see her daddy. Her father smiles as he looks at her, holding the ball behind his back. "Betty," he says, "Daddy bought you something very special today so that we can play together."

He takes the ball out from behind his back and says, "I'm going to teach you how to play catch." He tells her that once she learns how to play catch, they can have many fun times together. He says he always enjoyed playing catch with his father when his father came home from work. He became very good at catching the ball and as a result made many friends among other kids who liked to play ball. He tells her how important baseball was in his life, and how much he enjoyed playing it with his friends all through school.

Now Betty's father shows her the ball up close. "This is just a plastic baseball," he says, "but after you've practiced, maybe later on when you get a little older, I'll get you a real baseball. And maybe and even a glove and a bat."

Now, Betty may not understand everything that her daddy is telling her, but she is excited about the new toy he has given her. She recognizes that it is very important to him. He has her full attention.

Betty's father tells her to take a couple of steps back, saying "I'm going to toss the ball to you. You catch it and toss it back to me!" Very carefully, he tosses the ball to her, almost putting it directly in her hands. But as fate would have it, Betty drops the ball. Her father's face fills with disappointment. He shakes his head and he says, "I should have known that you would take after your mother's side of the family! Your mother isn't any good at this kind of thing either."

Instantly, Betty is crushed. Her eyes fill with tears. Her daddy tries tossing the ball to her again, and sure enough, with all hope gone and her eyes welling up with tears, she again drops it. She gives up and her father gives up. The message has been transmitted and received—there's something wrong with Betty.

After that, when Betty and her father are together in the toy store and she sees a ball, does she say, "Look, Daddy, a ball! Let's play catch!"?

No, that isn't very likely. She "knows" she isn't any good at playing catch—after all, her father told her so. The seed of inadequacy planted by her father's unthinking remark and her negative expectation of success may turn into a self-fulfilling prophesy. If she ever tries to play catch again, the belief that there's something wrong with her only increases the chances that she will fail, thus reinforcing her mistaken belief.

Now imagine that Betty catches the ball. Her father beams with excitement. He praises her, saying, "I knew you could do it!" It doesn't matter if she misses the next toss. She has been successful at catching the ball once, so she will most likely keep trying. If she goes into a toy store with her father and sees a basket full of balls, she is much more likely to get excited and say, "Look, Daddy. There's a ball! Let's play catch!"

Now let's start over one more time. Imagine she misses the ball. But this time, Daddy makes it his mistake, saying, "I was too far away" or "Oops, I didn't show you how to catch it yet—let's do it again!" Her father's reaction lets Betty know that it's okay to try something new, even if she doesn't do it exactly right the first time.

You can see that the effect of this event doesn't hinge on whether or not Betty catches the ball, but rather how the event effects her perceptions about herself—perceptions based on the reactions of someone important to her, her daddy.

Remember the Seething Cauldron of Emotions we talked

about earlier? Negative beliefs from the past about whether we are good enough can provide a lot of fuel under that cauldron. As in the first scenario with Betty, such beliefs can be generated by our interpretation of an event in the past and the way we feel about it. *Whenever we feel inadequate as adults, feelings from the past cascade into the present, compounding the effects and causing us to over-react.* Not only that, they can create anxiety regarding future events.

As adults, our feelings of inadequacy often revolve around our work. We may not feel we have performed at the level required. Someone, either a coworker or a supervisor, may have actually told us we need to do better in a certain area. Or we may be confronted by the need to do something we have never done before, such as learn a new computer program or develop a new skill.

In either case, feelings of inadequacy may lead us to avoid situations and opportunities that would enrich our lives. They can even be paralyzing, keeping us from taking the actions we know are crucial. Clearly, acknowledging and releasing self-defeating beliefs from the past can go a long way toward relieving our feelings of inadequacy in the present. And the more adequate we feel in managing our life situations, the more successful we will be.

Doing 1-2-3 with "Feeling Inadequate"

1. Identify/name the feeling: Inadequate or another name for inadequate that expresses a particular level of intensity, such as dumb, stupid, foolish, not good enough, inept, flawed.

2. Identify the cause of the feeling: Usually caused by an event in the present in which you felt some degree of failure to perform, which then resonates with negative programming from the past about not being good enough.

3. Identify a satisfying response: Satisfying responses to to the feeling of inadequacy fall into two categories.

   a. Do a reality check. Are you really inadequate, or do you need to change your perception of your performance?

   b. Recognize if there's an area in your life where you would be well-served to get or enhance certain skills.

   c. If you need to enhance your skills, plan how you will accomplish that.

Like most people, you probably find it difficult to separate your feelings about being worthy or good enough from your abilities and accomplishments. That's because you learned to connect the two very early on in your life. When you don't perform up to expectations, you feel like there's something wrong with you, that deep down, you aren't good enough. That belief can be so pervasive that you sometimes don't feel good enough no matter how much you accomplish, which is irrational.

But early in your life, there was a time when you didn't feel inadequate. That's a learned belief—and it can be unlearned. *Make it a practice to reject negative thoughts when they come. A friend of mind always says, "Cancel, cancel," when he wants to erase a negative thought. Then, replace the negative thought with*

a more realistic and positive thought or perception. If the effects of feeling inadequate are pervasive in your life, you may find it useful to get professional help, preferably someone who is trained in using the secret language of feelings and can teach you 7th Path Self-Hypnosis. But there's a lot you can do on your own by simply watching your internal dialogue.

It may also be difficult for you to separate an event happening in the present from the cascade of feelings from the past. This is especially true If you're caught in the mire of self-defeating beliefs. In that case, it can be helpful to talk to someone you trust in order to check your perceptions. He or she may be able to help you separate the present-time issue from perceptions based in the past. You can also do this for yourself by journaling, putting what actually happened on one side of the page and all the things you're telling yourself about what happened on the other side of the page

Once present-time events/perceptions are separated from beliefs/emotions generated from the past, you can be realistic about the many things you do competently. You can acknowledge that you have many skills and you can learn many more. Once you have done that, if there's a real need to enhance your work skills, for example, you will be in a much better position to do so.

1-2-3 Worksheet: Inadequate

In your **1-2-3** notebook, write down your responses to the following steps. The more specific you can be, the more useful your notebook will be in helping you create a satisfying life, both now and in the future.

Step 1. Identify/name the feeling. "Inadequate" or another name for inadequate that expresses a particular level of intensity, such as dumb, stupid, foolish, not good enough, inept, flawed, etc.

Step 2. Identify the cause. The perception that you're lacking in some important area of your life. Complete the sentence: Sometimes (or often) I feel inadequate when_____.

Step 3. List some satisfying responses. Follow the outline below as a guide for developing satisfying responses. Add resources and people who will support you in meeting your needs.

    A. Do a reality check. Am you really inadequate, or do you need a change of perspective?

    B. If you need a change of perspective, how can you develop one?

    C. If you need to get new skills or enhance others, how can you do that?

    D. Choose a practice will help you erase negative self-statements and make it part of your life.

Stress is just another form of fear—in this case, it's the fear that you won't get everything done well enough.

Chapter 12

The Wisdom of Feeling Stressed

Stress is the voice inside of you saying, "I feel like I have too much to do."

Stress seems to be unavoidable in our busy lives. We all feel it at some time or another, to some degree or another. There are multiple possible causes of stress, including unsatisfied Primary Feelings (internal stress), the external situation at the moment (situational stress), learned patterns of stress and emotional resonance with the past—as well as a combination of all of the above! It's important to listen to your feelings when you're stressed and then ask yourself, "What's happening in my life to cause this stress?" If you don't, you'll only experience the stress without understanding what you can do to alleviate it. Then you'll experience the desire to engage in some kind of distractor.

We've already discussed steps you can take to resolve the general feeling of stress coming from unsatisfied Primary Feelings.

Now it's time to look at a more specific kind of stress, the stress that can be generated by a specific situation in your life. This is the stress that you experience when you feel overwhelmed by your job, family or other responsibilities. The task before you seems too big to handle—or to handle well enough. It seems that there's simply too much to do and not enough resources, help or time available to get it done.

Stress is just another form of fear telling you, "I'm afraid something bad might happen if I don't get everything done well enough." It motivates you to do what needs to be done in order to reduce or eliminate the chance of being hurt, such as finding ways to reduce your commitments, get help or make use of available resources.

You've probably anticipated that the first step when feeling stressed is to do a reality check. Take the time to look at the situation and ask yourself, "Do I really have too much to do?" The answer might be a resounding "Yes!" In that case, you need to take action that will relieve you of some of your obligations.

On the other hand, you might do a reality check and discover that you really don't have too much to do. Your stress might be the result of poor time management, lack of organization or negative self-talk. In that case, the cause of stress can be addressed by learning—and putting into practice—skills leading to more effective organization and time management. Fortunately, there are many seminars and good books available on these topics. One of my favorites is "The Seven Habits of Highly Effective People" by

Stephen Covey.

Another possible result of your reality check might be that you see you're over-reacting, making a mountain out of a molehill. If this is the case, the satisfying response is to change your perspective. When you recognize that you really can handle your responsibilities—and begin to see your circumstances in this new way—the stress might disappear altogether! At the very least, it'll become much easier to manage.

Learning to Say "No"

Situational stress caused by actually having too many commitments can be exacerbated by the inability to "just say no" to a request. We like to feel useful. It feels wonderful to contribute and to be a person others can rely on to get things done. But there has to be a limit to what we take on, otherwise everything suffers.

Many people find it particularly difficult to say "no" if the request has been made by a supervisor or boss. In today's pared-down workplace, employees are routinely asked to take on projects that will be too much for them to handle, given their prior commitments. If this is your situation, you need to find a way to communicate to your boss that while you want to help, the circumstances are such that the new project is either not going to get done on time, or that doing it on time will negatively impact other current projects.

Talking to your boss in this way may be a new thing for you.

You might be feeling anxious just thinking about it. Try practicing what you'll say before you approach him or her. You might say something like this: "I think that project sounds really interesting and I would love to help you out by taking it on. But I'll need some direction from you regarding which of my other obligations can be put on the back burner."

The inability to limit what you're willing to commit to is often rooted in a lack of self-worth, fear of rejection, or fear of conflict. If you feel that your opinion isn't likely to be respected, or that your opinion doesn't count, you'll find it very difficult to say "no." In that case, personal work on self-esteem, as well as your ability to assert your thoughts and feelings about things, can give you the confidence you need.

To summarize, current (situational) stress can be the result of poor time-management or organizational skills, a lack of perspective, or not being able to say "no." Sometimes, however, the experience of stress has very little to do with what's going on in the present. Feeling stressed out all of the time can be learned, and the family often is the source of habitual, learned stress.

Habitual Stress

There are several possible underlying messages in families living with perpetual stress. In some families, the belief is that if you aren't stressed then you're not trying hard enough, or you don't really care. The message in other families is that the world is dangerous and you can never really do enough to be completely safe. This leads to hyper-vigilance, that is, being on high alert at all times. Still other families always seem to be in catastrophe mode, going from one unmanageable drama to the next. The message here is that no matter how hard you try, life will always somehow find a way to pull the rug out from under you. This kind of thinking leads to a life of ongoing unmanageable stress, which is inadvertently passed from parent to child and from generation to generation, over and over again.

I believe that anxiety disorders can easily be passed on from generation to generation, without any kind of genetic component. If you grew up in an environment where your parents were always a day late and a dollar short, always in a frenzy about how to handle even everyday situations, it's likely that you picked up that kind of behavior from them. If you don't learn to respond to stress in a different way than you may have learned as a child, you not only can pass it on to your children, it can even become a family tradition, so to speak.

Finally, your stress might be the result of simply over-reacting to what's going on in your life. You might not be consciously in a pattern of "catastrophic thinking," however. The source of your stress might be completely subconscious and a result of emotional resonance. Yes, it's back to the Seething Caldron of Emotions! *If you're carrying a lot of unsatisfied emotions about the past, or if you're worried about something in the future, even normal everyday responsibilities can cause you to boil over.*

Doing 1-2-3 with "Feeling Stressed"

1. Identify/name the feeling: Stressed out or another name that expresses a particular level of intensity such as overwhelmed, out of control.

2. Identify the cause of the feeling: Thinking you have too many things to do and not enough resources or help to do them well.

3. Identify a satisfying response: Below is a short outline of the steps you can take to determine what kind of response to feeling stressed will be satisfying.

> A. Do a reality check. Is your perception of the situation accurate. Do you really have too much to do?
> B. If the answer is "no," you'll feel less stressed right way.
> C. If the answer is "yes," create a plan for reducing stress, then follow it.

When you do the reality check, really be honest about what your situation is. Do you really have too much to do? Or is it more a matter of perception, perhaps brought on by being too tired? Is the situation a short-term, unavoidable pile-up of family and work obligations, or a chronic overload?

If you really do have too much to do and are suffering from chronic overload, it's time to take the actions necessary to create balance in your life. Answering the following questions can help you come up with ideas for satisfying responses.

The Wisdom of Feeling Stressed

Are you taking on something that a coworker, spouse or child is responsible for, either because you fear they won't do it or won't do it well enough? Are you taking on something that a coworker, spouse or child is responsible for, because you want to look good and be liked? Are you saying "yes" when you should be saying "no" because you don't like to disappoint people?

If you answered "yes" to any of the above questions, you might find it helpful to read one of the books that have been written on the subject of codependence. Do some work around recognizing that your self-worth doesn't depend on making others happy or getting their approval. Give the tasks back to the person they belong to. It's the best thing to do for both you and them, and it allows you to take on a more appropriate role, perhaps of being friend, manager or teacher.

Again, if you answered "yes," consider whether you've set standards that are unreachable, no matter how many hours you put in. Do you worry about not looking good if you don't stick to those standards? Remember what you read in the previous chapter on inadequacy about the need to separate accomplishments from the feeling of self worth. Let go of your fear of not looking good. Recognize that things don't have to be done perfectly to be done. They don't have to be done your way to be done. Delegate some tasks or better yet, create a team of people to help you with a project. You might discover that working together can create a sense of community you've been missing.

If your reality check revealed that you don't really have too much to do, your stress may be generated by poor organizational skills or procrastination. If that's the case, take a class or read a book for hints on how to manage your time, tasks and resources. Learn to prioritize. Determine what's really important and do the most important things first. Plan your work and work your plan—you'll be surprised at how freeing that is!

1-2-3 Worksheet: Stress

In your **1-2-3** notebook, write down your responses to the following steps. The more specific you can be, the more useful your notebook will be in helping you create a satisfying life, both now and in the future.

Step 1. Identify/name the feeling. Stressed out or another name that expresses a particular level of intensity such as overwhelmed, out of control.

Step 2. Identify the cause. You're thinking you have too many things to do and not enough resources or help to do them well. Write down how this shows up in your life.

Step 3. List some satisfying responses. In order to help you identify what responses will be truly satisfying, follow the outline below.

> A. Do a reality check. Is your perception accurate? Do you really have too much to do?
>
> B. If you answered "yes," answer the following questions:
> - What things can be done by someone else?
> - What things can be done less often or not at all?
> - Who are the people I can call on to support me in making changes in my priorities?
>
> C. Create a priority list and a plan. Be sure to schedule in time for yourself. Make a commitment to follow your plan and find a buddy who will hold you accountable.

All emotion comes from perception.
Fear comes from the perception of danger,
whether the danger is real or not.

Chapter 13

The Wisdom of Feeling Fearful

Fear is a voice inside of you saying, "I think something bad is going to happen."

I have saved the feeling of fear for the last among the Primary Feelings, because it is really the root of every other feeling that I have mentioned. When you aren't meeting your needs, then you don't feel totally safe and secure—and that generates fear.

None of us likes to feel afraid, and we especially don't like to admit it if we do! That is why we have so many other expressions for the feeling of fear, such as being anxious, nervous, worried, insecure, unsure, and so on. *Like all the Primary Feelings, fear is good, because it lets you know that you need to take care of yourself and the people in your life. It's like a voice saying, "You need to take action."*

We who live in stable countries and have our basic needs for food and shelter met may rarely feel fear as the result of a life-threatening situation. When we do, it's often because of something unexpected, such as an accident, illness or natural disaster. The actions fear prompts us to take in those situations are actions that will increase our probability for survival. If there aren't any actions we can take to change things, our fear can be accompanied by a feeling of frustration. We're then called upon to develop healthy coping strategies to deal with a situation that is largely out of our control.

For most of us, however, the fear we experience is the result of not having our emotional needs met. When we aren't meeting our needs, we don't feel totally safe and secure, which generates a state of fear. If we're only slightly afraid, we might say we're "concerned." If the fear is stronger, we might use the word "anxious" or "worried" to express how we feel. Here are some examples of the connection between fear and human needs.

> Sadness is generated when you're afraid that the loss of an important person or thing will leave you unable to satisfy some need. (People and things are important to you for the very reason that they help you to fulfill a need, want or desire.)

> Stress is generated when you're afraid that you won't get things done, or done well enough.

> If you're bored, you're afraid that your life will be wasted, or that it will be meaningless, or that you're unimportant.

If you feel lonely, you're afraid you will never have meaningful relationships, perhaps that you will never have a significant other and/or children. Or the lack of companionship may make you feel vulnerable.

As you can see from the above examples, **fear can be identified as the root cause of all the discomfort or emotional pain that we experience**. Because it's the root cause, the message fear has for us is very important. It's the great motivator and teacher—if we know how to decipher its message. If we don't, we remain stuck in our pain or in the frustrating cycle of distraction.

Blessing the Pain

Once I was visited by someone I consider to be a great spiritual teacher. This teacher said to me, "Bless the pain." At first I didn't understand what he was saying. I thought it might be one of those spiritual truths that are difficult to grasp, one that I might have to spend the rest of my life contemplating. I asked, "Why?" and the response changed my life. "Because," said the teacher, "it points away from itself."

Those few words really encapsulate what the secret language of feelings is all about. **Emotional pain (fear) is the great teacher. It points away from itself to what needs to be done for a satisfying response.** Its purpose is to help and guide us toward a more satisfying life.

I was once sitting with some Ishaya monks who were

answering questions from a group of Ascension practitioners. (Ascension is a meditation-like practice that focuses on praise, gratitude, love and compassion. It's designed to awaken the practitioner to "full human consciousness" and bring enlightenment.) One of the student practitioners asked, "If I believe in reincarnation, why should I practice daily meditation? I'll get another chance in my next life!"

For some reason, I felt moved to speak up. I asked the student, "How much pain do you want?"

That's a question worth asking yourself as you read this book. Pain points away from itself to some needed action. *If we attempt to ignore the pain or distract from it—and therefore don't take the action leading to a satisfying response—we will continue to experience the pain*, sometimes for years, as in the case of chronic sorrow or guilt. Not only that, we will most likely also experience the downward cycle of frustration and depression.

On the other hand, through experiencing our emotions, really feeling them, and applying the **1-2-3** of the secret language of feelings, we can move through pain and create more fulfilling lives. So, how much pain do you want?

Deprogramming Habitual Fear

Remember that fear is good, in that it's there to let you know that you need to take care of yourself and the people in your life. It's like a voice saying, "You need to take action." However, sometimes there's actually nothing in our situation to be afraid of—we're only reacting to a habit of feeling afraid all the time. Or something harmless in our present may be triggering an old fear from the past through emotional resonance.

If you have determined that there really is no significant danger generating the fear that you're experiencing, that fear is an internal stressor. It's the result of old programming, habitual negative thought patterns or traumatic experiences from the past. Fortunately, there are some steps you can take to reprogram your thoughts.

As I've mentioned before, one of the first things you can do is to start becoming aware of your "self-talk," i.e., the commentary that is continually running in your mind. We all tend to run the same thoughts through our minds over and over again. That constant repetition of thoughts either reinforces or weakens the programming that we carry inside ourselves.

If your habitual thoughts are primarily negative or fearful, you need to start deprogramming yourself right away. Many self-help books move directly into reprogramming through affirmations, but **unless the old, habitual thoughts are deprogrammed, any new suggestions for successful, satisfying behavior changes will be automatically rejected.**

A simple first step to take in deprogramming habitual fearful thoughts is to realize that **not every thought that goes through your head is true.** Habitual, automatic thoughts are the result of the decisions we made about how life is, often when we were very small. These decisions became beliefs generating thoughts and actions which at one time helped you cope.

Now, however, the coping mechanism that helped keep you safe or made you feel safe in the past may be creating the negative effects you see in your life—without you being consciously aware of it! Practice being aware of some of the 50,000 thoughts you have every day.

1. Recognize that you aren't your thoughts.
2. Acknowledge habitual negative or fearful thoughts with "Thank you for sharing!" or some other phrase.
3. Replace negative thoughts with positive or more realistic thoughts.

Becoming aware of and releasing thoughts that don't serve you is a very helpful practice. When you take those simple steps, you avoid adding emotional energy to your old habitual thoughts and old programming. This is easier said than done, but can make a big difference.

You can also use journaling to identify negative programming. Set up the journal so that you write whatever comes into your mind on one side of the page—the "good," the "bad" and the "ugly." Use the other side of the page to identify the beliefs associated with your thoughts. This practice can be very enlightening, especially when taken on over an extended period of time. You can also use that side of the page to question whether your habitual thoughts/beliefs are based in reality or are the result of something you decided about life when you were very young.

Challenging Your Beliefs

The following Challenge is a powerful way to deprogramming habitual thoughts, i.e. fears, you have identified in your journal. It has been modified from the Life Skills Coaching Script that the Rapid Eye Institute of Salem, Oregon, includes in its training manuals. Similar approaches are also often used in coaching and psychotherapy. Here is the structure for the Challenge:

- Identify the **event** that triggered the "bad" feeling.

- Identify the **habitual thought or limiting belief** associated with the feeling. See example below.

  > If_____doesn't happen, I'll never
  > have (or be)_____ again.
  > (If Joe doesn't ask me out, I'll never be happy
  > again!")

- Identify the **feelings and behaviors (distractors)** that the belief generates.

- Challenge the belief by asking, "What evidence do I have that this is true?"

- Create a rational new belief by answering the question, "What other way can I look at this situation?" Ex.: "If Joe doesn't call, I'll be really disappointed, but I'll find someone else to spend the evening with."

The above suggestions for deprogramming are practices you do using your conscious mind. They work, especially if you're ready to make a change. But they can take a long time.

There are also ways to deprogram that work with the subconscious mind for powerful and fast results. For example, hypnosis with a properly trained and certified hypnotherapist (preferably one who knows the secret language of feelings) can help you move along much more quickly by working with the subconscious mind to remove barriers to success.

In addition, you might consider using the special kind of self-hypnosis called 7th Path™ Self Hypnosis. This process allows you to release or neutralize the old emotions which are stressing your system and creating additional stress by resonating with situations in the present. Teachers and therapists trained in 7th Path™ are experienced in using the secret language of feelings. See the Appendix for information on hypnotists in your area who are trained in 7th Path™.

Doing 1-2-3 with "Feeling Fearful"

1. Identify/name the feeling: Afraid or fear by another name that expresses a particular level of intensity such as anxious, worried, nervous, insecure, frightened, scared to death, etc.

2. Identify the cause of the feeling: You're thinking that something bad might happen to you or someone you care about.

3. Identify a satisfying response: Evaluate the situation by doing a reality check to see if there's really a danger. Depending on the individual's situation, danger can be anything from imminent physical threat to worry about taking a test. Fear can range from worry about looking foolish to fear of injury or death. Regardless of the degree of danger or fear, **if there's a real threat, take action. If there's something you can do to prepare for the situation, begin to do it.** Get the information you need. Get the resources, including support from those around you.

If you can avoid the threat by getting away and staying away from certain situations and people, do so. Note that this isn't the same as copping out or avoiding a situation that requires you to perform at a level that is a little scary, such as taking on a new assignment, singing in public for the first time or putting yourself on the line in some essentially positive way. This kind of avoidance also isn't to be confused with distracting yourself in order to avoid challenge in your life.

If the situation or threat is of such a nature that it can neither be avoided nor handled successfully (a terminal illness, for example), draw on all your resources to make the best of the situation. Create a plan of action that will be satisfying, even though there will not be a good outcome.

On the other hand, if your reality check indicates that there's no real danger or that the probability is extremely low, then there will be an instant reduction in fear. When you catch yourself in the pattern of habitual negative and fearful thoughts even though there's no threat, do one of the following:

Remind yourself, "My worries and fears aren't based in reality."

Begin the practice of letting your thoughts go with a phrase such as "Thank you for sharing."

Use the Challenge to gain a more realistic picture of your situation.

Consciously replace negative thoughts with a phrase that empowers you.

1-2-3 Worksheet: Fear

In your **1-2-3** notebook, write down your responses to the following steps. The more specific you can be, the more useful your notebook will be in helping you create a satisfying life, both now and in the future.

Step 1. Identify the feeling. Afraid or fear by another name that expresses a particular level of intensity such as anxious, worried, nervous, insecure, frightened, scared to death, etc.

Step 2. Identify the cause. You're thinking that something bad might happen to you or someone you care about. Describe the perceived danger.

Step 3. List some satisfying responses. In order to help you identify what responses will be truly satisfying, follow the outline below.

    A. Do a reality check. Is the situation really dangerous?

    B. If the situation isn't dangerous, find a practice that will help you change your perception and/or consider sessions with a qualified professional.

    C. If there is a real danger present, plan on another sheet how you will do one or more of the following:
- Prepare for it.
- Avoid it.
- Make the best of it.

*Frustration is often confused with anger,
but anger comes for the perception of unfairness
and frustration comes from not being able to
meet your needs, wants and desires.*

Chapter 14

The Wisdom of Feeling Frustrated

Frustration is a voice inside saying, "What I'm doing isn't working!"

All of the feelings we've done *1-2-3* with so far are Primary Feelings as defined in this book. Now it's time to turn our attention to the Secondary Feeling of Frustration and the Tertiary Feeling of Depression.

Because it's so important to recognize the cycle of behavior that results in frustration and depression, let's review how it works. We'll begin at the point of the cycle when we notice that we "feel bad." At that point, we may or may not have identified exactly what the "bad" feeling is—we may just be aware that we feel uneasy or irritated.

If our reaction to "feeling bad" is to distract from it, the unmet need our feeling points to remains unmet—and the feeling intensifies. If we're taking action to fill the need and are

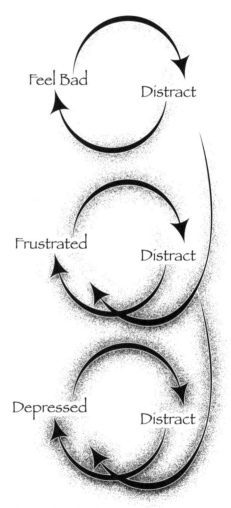

Figures 5 The Feel Bad/Distract/Frustrated/Depressed Cycle

unsuccessful, the feeling intensifies. Either way, as the need goes unmet, the feeling intensifies. Plus, we become frustrated, because what we're doing isn't working.

At this point we might tell someone, "I feel like I'm hitting my head against a brick wall!" That's a clear indication that we need to do something different than what we've been doing. If we continue our unsatisfying behavior—distracting or the unsuccessful attempt to meet the need—both the Primary Feeling and the frustration grow in intensity.

Over a period of time, the Primary Feeling and our frustration at not being able to satisfy our needs can intensify to the point of being intolerable. When the pain we're suffering becomes greater than our nervous systems can tolerate, the body kicks in with the Tertiary Feeling in our model, depression. Depression says, "I need to take a break before trying again." **When we stop trying to satisfy the need, want or desire generating the pain of the Primary Feeling, our feelings of frustration will immediately begin to fade. However, our need still remains unmet.**

As you look at Figure 5, you're probably thinking that it makes a lot of sense to do some **1-2-3** self-coaching when you first become aware of a painful Primary Feeling. Once you get used to paying attention to how you're feeling, you'll find you can do **1-2-3** quite quickly, especially if you've taken the time to fill out the worksheets at the end of the previous chapters in Part Two. As you make **1-2-3** an ongoing practice, you'll find that you spend much less time feeling frustrated and depressed.

That is the magic of learning and using the **1-2-3** of the secret language of feelings. Practicing **1-2-3** not only greatly reduces the intensity of the emotional pain you're feeling, but also the amount of time you spend in emotional pain. As a result, you spend more time involved in doing things that truly satisfy your needs, wants and desires. You become a much happier and more successful person.

Frustration: A Call for Change

Frustration isn't just an increase in the intensity of the pain experienced as the Primary Feeling. When you experience frustration, the need that isn't being met is **the need to be able to fulfill your needs, wants and desires through your own effort.** When you're unable to satisfy your needs through your own efforts, it shakes your feeling of security and your sense of being able to be effective in your environment. This in turn generates a particular kind of fear, which is what frustration is.

There are only two ways to end frustration. The first and most desirable way is to find a satisfying response to the Primary Feeling. Because such a response satisfies your need, it relieves the unpleasant Primary Feeling. Because what you're doing is now working, it also relieves the Secondary Feeling of frustration.

The second way to end frustration is to simply stop trying. In that case, you'll still experience the Primary Feeling, but at least it will not be exacerbated by frustration. If you're lonely, for example, and you give up and stop trying, you'll no longer feel lonely and frustrated—you'll only feel lonely.

This is why many people give up and stop trying to satisfy a particular need. They find not trying is less painful than trying and experiencing the frustration of being unsuccessful. And, **under certain circumstances, their decision to stop trying may be the correct thing to do, at least until an effective and appropriate action can be found.** If they keep doing what they have been doing, it almost guarantees more frustration leading to depression.

Once we understand the meaning of the feeling we call frustration, we'll spend much less time in this painful state. That's because whenever we start feeling frustrated, we'll recognize it's as a red flag telling us that our actions (responses) aren't effective at satisfying our needs. With this kind of awareness, we can immediately stop the frustrating behavior and consider what we need to do next. We can then begin to generate alternative approaches.

Frustration is almost always a call for creativity. Either we must become more creative ourselves in coming up with ways to satisfy our need, or we can borrow the creativity of another (i.e., ask for advice, take a class, read a book, etc.).

Doing 1-2-3 with "Feeling Frustrated"

1. Identify/name the feeling: Frustrated or another name that expresses a particular level of intensity such as irritated, blocked, thwarted, disappointed, confused, defeated, etc.

2. Identify the cause of the feeling: You're either distracting from an unpleasant feeling or trying unsuccessfully to meet your needs—and what you have been doing isn't satisfying.

3. Identify a satisfying response: In the case of frustration, you won't be looking for a satisfying response to the frustration itself. Instead, you'll first identify the Primary Feeling that came before the frustration, and then identify an action that satisfies the need indicated by that Primary Feeling. When the need is met, the feeling of frustration is relieved.

Sometimes, your frustration can be so intense that you're more aware of it than the Primary Feeling underlying it. If that's the case, you might need to do a little investigating. In this scenario, you start with the frustration and work backwards to the Primary feeling. Ask yourself, "What action is causing my frustration? What is it that I'm trying to accomplish? What need am I trying to fill?" Once you have a sense of the need you're trying to fill, you'll be pretty clear about what the Primary Feeling is.

If you're already clear about what the Primary Feeling is, you probably won't have much trouble identifying the unmet need. Then you can investigate why doing what you're doing isn't working. It might be that you really aren't putting your full effort and commitment behind taking the action that will make a difference. Maybe you aren't being consistent in your efforts. Maybe the idea for satisfying your need is appropriate, but could be more effectively implemented by some slight changes.

More often, you'll discover that you need to change your approach. ***Remember that frustration isn't necessarily a call for doing more of whatever you have been doing—more often, it's a demand that you DO SOMETHING ELSE!*** Trying harder at what doesn't work isn't only a waste of effort, it's a guarantee of failure. Most of us have heard this definition of being crazy: Doing the same thing over and over again—and expecting a different result!

Now that you're looking for creative solutions, consider getting friends together for a brainstorming session. Or join a group that is focusing on the same issue. Read some of the self-help books that are currently available. Take a class. Try something outrageously different, something you wouldn't have even considered doing before. Sometimes that's the best way to break out of a pattern.

1-2-3 Worksheet: Frustrated

In your **1-2-3** notebook, write down your responses to the following steps. The more specific you can be, the more useful your notebook will be in helping you create a satisfying life, both now and in the future.

Step 1. Identify the feeling. Frustrated or another name that expresses a particular level of intensity such as irritated, blocked, thwarted, disappointed, confused, defeated, etc.

Step 2. Identify the cause. You're either 1) distracting from an unpleasant feeling or 2) trying unsuccessfully to meet your needs. Either way, what you have been doing isn't meeting your needs. Be specific about how it shows up in your life.

Step 3. List some satisfying responses. In order to help you identify what responses will be truly satisfying, follow the outline below.

> A. Do a reality check. Are your perceptions about the results you're getting accurate?
>
> B. What Primary need, want or desire isn't being satisfied?
>
> C. Look at the worksheet you filled out for that Primary Feeling to see what actions you have listed under Step 3. Pick one or two and list them below—then do them! Remember—frustration is a call to do something different!

Chapter 15

The Wisdom of Feeling Depressed

Depression is a voice inside of you saying "I quit —it hurts too much to continue to try anymore."

Remember earlier in this book when I tried to explain to my friend that all feelings were good? He was unable to accept the idea that there might be something good about feeling angry. I've also run across a lot of resistance to the idea that there could be something good about feeling depressed.

That resistance may be due to the fact that there are extreme levels of depression that require medical intervention. **To avoid any misunderstanding as we discuss this topic, I want to emphasize that if a person is in a dangerous level of depression, such that he or she may hurt themselves or someone else, certainly steps need to be taken to ensure everyone's safety.** An individual in such a situation might need to be hospitalized and/or receive medication, preferably cared for by medical professionals who understand the secret language of feelings and hold the possibility that the individual might eventually be able to stop taking medication.

That having been said, my belief is that otherwise normal and healthy people who periodically experience feeling "down" or "low" can learn to understand and use the feeling of depression to their advantage. As a result of using the **1-2-3** of the secret language of feelings, they'll spend much less time feeling depressed and much more time feeling good. Why? Because they'll have learned to fulfill their needs, wants and desires. This is a much more positive approach to depression than taking unnecessary medications.

Frustration and Depression

In the previous chapter, we reviewed the "Feel Bad/Frustrated/Depressed" cycle, which begins with a need being unsatisfied. This unsatisfied need generates the emotional pain of a Primary Feeling. When the attempt to satisfy the need is unsuccessful, a new dose of pain is served up from the nervous system—the Secondary Feeling of frustration. This frustration can only be reduced or eliminated by satisfying the need, want or desire, or by ending efforts to satisfy it by giving up trying.

As long as an individual tries to satisfy the Primary Feeling and continues to be unsuccessful, the feeling of frustration will intensify. Remember that effort is required to experience frustration, and that continued effort without success increases the intensity of the frustration. This is very important in understanding the meaning of feeling depressed.

Frustration is an internal stress that is caused by unsuccessful efforts to satisfy a need. If you continue in the cycle of effort followed by lack of success, the ever-increasing frustration—and ever-increasing stress—will begin to affect your health. **The Tertiary Feeling of depression is the safety valve nature has provided to save you from the continuing fruitless effort in which you were engaged.** The feeling of depression says, "Stop trying. It's not working. Quit until you can come up with something that might work."

The cycle of effort leading to depression is equivalent to an automobile spinning its wheels on a slippery surface. It's going nowhere, only burning up fuel and wearing out the motor and other moving parts. At that point, it's best to turn off the car and see if something else can be done—in other words, stop trying! Even if some alternate action comes to mind, the overheated motor may need to cool off for awhile and fuel or oil reserves may need to be replenished. The same can be said for us when we're highly frustrated. It's time to take a rest, cool down and replenish ourselves.

If we looked at depression the same way we look at taking a break from spinning a car's wheels, our response would be quite different than it has been in the past. Rather than denying the way we feel and attempting to continue our lives as if nothing were wrong (taking medications for depression or distracting ourselves with food and drugs, etc.), we could allow ourselves to step back and perhaps unplug for awhile to rest and replenish.

While resting, we could begin to look at things from a different perspective, do some brainstorming for alternate actions, or get some help from someone else who has expertise regarding the issue that is frustrating us. First, however, we have to stop what we were doing.

The reason we stop trying after weeks and maybe months of effort is that we feel hopeless. It's important to note that as long as we're trying to satisfy our needs, we're in a state of hopefulness. We wouldn't even try to fill our needs if we thought our efforts were useless. However, when our efforts are not succeeding, the frustration becomes greater than our hopefulness. We start feeling like there's no reason to try any longer. We feel hopeless, and hopelessness depresses our motivation, leading to the inaction that marks depression.

Thus, **depression is best understood as a message of hopelessness.** Seen in this light, hope and depression are opposites. Being mutually exclusive, depression and hopefulness cannot both exist in the same place. This is why I often say to the helping professionals, "Stop treating depression!" **Depression is not the problem, it's only a symptom of the problem.** Instead, offer your clients hope. Offer them new ways that might help them fulfill their needs, wants, and desires.

How can professionals offer hope to those who are caught up

in the pain of depression? By asking them, "What were you frustrated about?" As they tell you about their frustration, they'll reveal the needs, wants and desires they were trying unsuccessfully to satisfy. Essentially, you can do **1-2-3** in reverse. If you can help them come up with more effective ways to satisfy their needs, wants and desires, you may kindle a feeling of hope inside of them. Hopefulness leads to action, and as the individuals learn to take more effective actions, the possibility exists of them satisfying their needs, wants and desires. This is the way to help individuals move from depression. It's a plan of action that can be taken whenever necessary with a high degree of success.

When you feel depressed, you can do the same for yourself. Just follow the **1-2-3** self-coaching below.

Doing 1-2-3 with "feeling depressed"

1. Identify/name the feeling: Depressed or another name that expresses a particular level of intensity such as down, in the dumps, in the doldrums, trapped, hopeless, etc. Often confused with feeling sad.

2. Identify the cause of the feeling: You are experiencing a level of frustration that is too much to handle, so you have to quit trying. The cause of the frustration, i.e., the Primary Feeling and unmet need that preceded it, is specific to your situation.

3. Identify a satisfying response: In the case of depression, it's very important to acknowledge what you are feeling, then give yourself permission to rest and replenish. (Again, this is an appropriate response to a level of depression that is normal for healthy individuals.)

When you are ready to try again, identify what was frustrating you. It's usually only one or two issues. You might do a drill such as:

- I was frustrated because I was trying to _____. (the goal you haven't been able to achieve).

- I was trying to do that, because I was feeling _____. (Primary Feeling)

- I was feeling_____ because I haven't been meeting my need for _____. (need, want or desire).

Once you have identified the unmet need that began this cycle and have acknowledged that what you were doing wasn't working, you can start coming up with possible new solutions. **Remember, recovery from depression requires both rest and a new approach.** It might be tempting to fall back into your old, familiar and ineffective behaviors, but please don't do it! That's just a first-class ticket back to frustration and depression.

Coming up with new ideas might not be as hard as you think. It's entirely possible that during your R & R period, your subconscious has been busy figuring out a whole list of satisfying responses! This is especially true if you were giving yourself a healthy, restful break—not wearing yourself out with feeling guilty for feeling depressed. Also, remember to get input from friends, clergy, books and any other resources available.

As you get ready to try again, review the chapter on frustration—because the minute you start to try again, you risk frustration again. But don't let the possibility of frustration keep you from trying. Frustration is good, it's a part of life. We try an action that we've identified as a satisfying response. If it works, great! If it doesn't and we get frustrated, our frustration is just an indication that we need to try something new. It's that light on the dashboard, telling us what we need in order to get the most out of our lives.

1-2-3 Worksheet: Depression

In your **1-2-3** notebook, write down your responses to the following steps. The more specific you can be, the more useful your notebook will be in helping you create a satisfying life, both now and in the future.

Step 1. Identify the feeling. "Depressed" or name that expresses a particular level of intensity such as feeling down, blue, in the doldrums, trapped, hopeless, etc.

Step 2. Identify the cause. What you're doing is not working, and the frustration you feel is so painful, you've quit trying. You feel hopeless—nothing will ever change. Be specific about how it shows up in your life.

Step 3. List some satisfying responses. In order to help you identify what responses will be truly satisfying, follow the outline below.

> A. Rest up. Take it easy, be kind to yourself. Get the support of your family and/or others for this little break in effort.
>
> B. When you're ready to try again, enlist the help of friends, a professional coach or a teacher. Brainstorm with them for new solutions or approaches to the issue you're working on.
>
> C. Step out again, and risk frustration in your attempt to fulfill your needs, wants and desires. Pay attention to what's working and what isn't—that will reduce the amount of time you spend feeling frustrated.

Chapter 16

The Wisdom of Feeling Sympathy

Sympathy can cause you to feel "bad" because someone else is hurting. It can also activate emotions from your past through emotional resonance.

In Chapter 5, I mentioned that in addition to the chapters on each of the Primary Feelings, I would have a chapter on sympathy. You might have wondered why. The answer is emotional resonance. When we feel sympathy for another's pain, we're motivated to help. Until we can separate our feelings and needs from the past from the feelings and needs of the other, it's difficult to recognize what response—if any—is appropriate.

According to the "Merriam-Webster Collegiate Dictionary," the word sympathy has Latin and Greek roots which mean "having common feelings." The definition states that sympathy is "the correlation existing between bodies capable of communicating their vibrational energy to one another through some medium."

Sounds a lot like emotional resonance, doesn't it? The difference is that rather than the emotional signal vibrating within one's own psyche from the past into the present moment, the experience of sympathy is a sympathetic vibration between two or more individuals. The "medium" is the social connection we experience with others.

The ability to experience sympathy—or emotional resonance—demonstrates to us that we do have a social connection to others that's very real, especially in regards to those we're closest to and care most about. This connection allows us to function in a positive way in our society. In fact, the lack of a social connection is debilitating enough to be listed as a symptom of some mental disorders.

Sympathy, then, is useful because it motivates us to help others. It's an important part of being human and living together. Human beings may even be genetically programmed to help each other. Wouldn't it be in the best interest of the species to be helpful to one another, even in cases where there seems to be no direct benefit to the individual helping?

It's not surprising that we feel more sympathetic toward the people we care the most about. For example, consider the relationship between mother and child, which is perhaps the closest of all human relationships. The mother-child connection is so profound that it's almost certain a mother will feel sympathetic pain when an infant is in pain.

The Wisdom of Feeling Sympathy

This pain, emotional or physical or both, is obviously not the actual pain that the child is experiencing. It's a resonant pain activated through sympathy, and it motivates the mother to act in a way that helps her child—and in the big picture, the species in general.

In varying degrees, sympathy is generated by the level of love and caring we feel for the individuals in our lives. We more easily sympathize with our children than children of distant relatives. We tend to sympathize more with our close friends than with acquaintances, and more with our neighbors than with people across town or across the country.

The more we care about another person, the more we're likely to feel sympathetic pain in response to his or her pain. Caring is the medium in which the vibrations flow, and the sympathy we feel motivates us to act in the interest of others, especially those we love.

We also seem to be more prone to sympathize with those who appear to be most like us, who are of the same race, religion or nationality, than with others whom we perceive as being different from us.

As unfortunate as this seems, there may have been some inherent benefit genetically during the early history of man. But it isn't always a benefit. The ability to feel the pain of those who are like us has had both good and bad consequences throughout history, depending upon the viewpoint. It's caused both wars and peace. It's caused communities to either pull together or be pulled apart.

When someone else becomes afraid, either a person or a country, we either feel fearful ourselves, because the danger is there for us also, or we become afraid for them. The fear we feel motivates us to help them out, perhaps by helping them prepare for or avoid the dangerous circumstance.

In an example of sympathetic fear, let's say a big brother becomes aware that his little brother is scared of the neighborhood bully. He feels his little brother's fear, which motivates him to take action on behalf of his sibling. He informs the bully that he'll consider an attack on his little brother to be an attack on himself. The bully avoids the little brother from that time on.

Nations can bond together in much the same way, making contracts or treaties of mutual support against a perceived enemy— an attack against one nation becomes an attack against all of them.

So sympathy—feeling another's pain through emotional resonance—is good in that it motivates us to take care of one another. It's especially beneficial and appropriate when others are helpless, unable to do for themselves what needs to be done because of physical, social, economic or political inequity. In that case, sympathy and anger can motivate another to make the situation fair.

There are times, however, when we may be motivated by sympathy to act for others who are actually capable of doing what needs to be done themselves. What we're feeling in this case is a combination of interpersonal resonance with another—feeling their pain generated by unmet needs—plus emotional resonance with our own past. This potent mix can cause us to over-react to a situation which is primarily affecting another person.

For example, let's say a father with a history of being treated unfairly finds out his son is being treated in a similar way. This creates emotional resonance with the father's past. Feelings of anger, fear and frustration cascade into the present. He becomes overprotective of his son in an attempt to keep the son from experiencing the pain he experienced as a child.

While the father's motivation is love and the desire to protect his son from harm, such behavior is problematic for the child. He becomes fearful himself and overly dependent on his father. If this theme continues, the child will have difficulty maturing into a responsible adult, because he will not have experienced the normal painful events of life that can develop inner strength. It's through meeting the challenges of our lives that we grow as individuals and ultimately reach our potential as adults.

Now let's take a look at how you can use **1-2-3** to satisfy a feeling if it's caused by interpersonal resonance.

Doing 1-2-3 with "Feeling Sympathy"

1. Identify/name the feeling: Sympathy or sympathy by

another name that expresses a particular level of intensity such as being in tune with, feeling compassion for, etc.

2. Identify the cause of the feeling: You're experiencing emotional resonance with a person whom you perceive to be in emotional pain and therefore in need of something.

3. Identify a satisfying response: Do **1-2-3** on your own feelings. Then do a reality check to see if it's appropriate for you to take action on behalf of the other. If it's appropriate, work with the person to create a plan of action for satisfying his or her needs, wants and desires.

Doing **1-2-3** on what you're feeling is very important in this situation. Your feelings may be telling you that there's an unresolved issue in your past that must be taken care of. **If your desire to act is motivated by the emotional pressure of the past event, rather than the other person's true needs, it's probably inappropriate.** You're feeling that you need to take care of the other, when you really need to take care of yourself.

Next, do a reality check. Are your perceptions about the other person's emotional pain—and the cause of the pain—accurate? Is the person in any degree of danger or need that requires immediate response by someone else?

You can also do a reality check with the other person. Are her perceptions about her situation accurate? Is there another way to look at it? This can be especially helpful when the other person is a child or adolescent who doesn't have the benefit of life experience.

Please offer to do **1-2-3** with the individual. By teaching her this process, you give her the opportunity to identify responses that are satisfying to her. Plus, you give her a tool that she can use to learn how to be more effective in her own life.

Finally, if there's a basic need or imminent danger that must be responded to and you're the appropriate person to take action, by all means, take action! If the young, aged or helpless are in need, it's the right thing to do. The feeling of sympathy motivates us to act on behalf of another for the good of all.

1-2-3 Worksheet: Sympathy

In your **1-2-3** notebook, write down your responses to the following steps. The more specific you can be, the more useful your notebook will be in helping you create a satisfying life, both now and in the future.

Step 1. Identify the feeling. Sympathy or sympathy by another name that expresses a particular level of intensity such as being in tune with, feeling compassion for, etc.

Step 2. Identify the cause. you're experiencing emotional resonance with a person whom you perceive to be in emotional pain and therefore in need of something. Be specific about the person and the need.

Step 3. List some satisfying responses. Use the outline below as a guide to help you determine whether you should take action on behalf of the other person, focus on your own needs, or a combination of both.

> A. Do **1-2-3** on your own feelings using the appropriate worksheet. What about the other's situation has created emotional resonance? What needs, wants and desires do you need to satisfy?

> B. Do a reality check. Are your perceptions about the other's distress accurate? Is there an immediate need for action? Is it appropriate for you to act on the other's behalf?

> C. Assist the other in doing **1-2-3** on his or her feelings. Focus on a list of actions he or she can take, as well as resources and people who can help.

> D. Take action on behalf of the other, if appropriate.

Chapter 17

Feelings Can Occur in Combination

As you went through the chapters on the Primary Feelings, you probably wondered about all the times you felt as if you were caught in a whirlwind, experiencing many feelings at once. I've touched briefly on how feelings can occur in combination, such as in the chapter on sadness, but now it's time to go into it in more depth.

Two feelings that often occur together are sadness and loneliness. Remember Mary, who had lost her mother? She was experiencing sadness caused by her mother's passing. She was also experiencing loneliness caused by no longer having the person in her life who was satisfying her need for social contact.

Here we have two distinctly different feelings being generated by the same incident. Other incidents that could generate the same two feelings are the breakup of a couple, a friend moving to another state, or a misunderstanding that resulted in a break in communication. If any of these have happened to you, sadness was telling you that you needed to get back or replace the person you lost, because that person was important to you. Loneliness was telling you that you're no longer able to fulfill your social need for human companionship by having that person in your life.

When these two feelings are present at the same time, it's very likely they will provide double the motivation to regain the relationship, if that's possible. Of course this presupposes that the other person is willing and/or able to come back to you. If that's not possible, the two feelings work together to prompt you to develop an equally satisfying relationship with someone else.

As I mentioned earlier, you can be lonely for someone specific. If you're lonely for your spouse, being with your parents does not satisfy your need, want or desire. If you're sad about the loss of someone important, like a loved one, you may always feel somewhat sad about the loss, even though you have built a new and perhaps equally satisfying relationship. For example, a widow who has remarried may be totally committed to and completely in love with her new husband, yet still feel sad over the loss of her former husband whenever his memory comes up.

In the case of two Primary Feelings occurring together, you can do 1-2-3 with each feeling separately, since each feeling is the demand for a particular need to be met. If this sounds complicated, be assured that it is very doable! With practice, you'll soon be able to identify most Primary Feelings as being separate and distinct, even when they are occurring together.

Anger and Frustration

In cases when a Primary Feeling and the Secondary Feeling of frustration occur together, the task is to separate out the two and focus on the Primary Feeling. That sounds easy, but it can be a bit tricky when the Primary Feeling involved is anger. This is because anger and frustration can seem to be a great deal alike, which can cause some confusion when you're experiencing them. However, they are two distinct feelings. Anger, a Primary Feeling, comes from the perception of unfairness. Frustration, the single Secondary Feeling, comes from the perception that what you're doing isn't working. They often occur in conjunction, when an action we think *should* work doesn't work.

There are times when we know beforehand that the action we're about to undertake has the possibility of failure. For example, the standard procedure in your workplace might require that the least expensive course of action be tried first, even though the likelihood of success is rather low. Or, you might choose to try a procedure (or drug) that's unlikely to succeed, because it has a low occurrence of side effects compared to the procedure (drug) that's more likely to succeed. When you know beforehand that there's the likelihood of failure, you don't get angry when that turns out to be the case.

However, when you try something that you believe should work, a new dimension has been added—the "should." When you believe that what you're doing should work, but it doesn't, that seems unfair. You become angry. If you keep trying, you eventually are both angry and frustrated. The feeling of anger is saying that the situation isn't fair, because what you're doing should work! The feeling of frustration is telling you that what you're doing isn't working and you need to try something else.

The first step when feelings are occurring in combination is to separate out the Primary Feeling and do 1-2-3 self-coaching with it. After naming the feeling (in this case, anger) and identifying the cause (perception of unfairness), do a reality check. Is the situation really unfair? The response you choose will be different depending upon whether it is or not.

It may take some practice to differentiate between anger and frustration and their messages. Once you begin to do so, you'll hear anger saying, "This should work! It isn't fair that it's not going the way it should go!" You'll hear frustration saying, "Be creative, look at this problem from a different angle, get someone else's point of view on the subject." If you respond appropriately to each of the messages, you'll begin to find your way out of anger and frustration much more quickly.

Sometimes when we're angry and frustrated, we're also tired, and the anger has come after a series of unsuccessful tries. In situations like this, if you can just take a break, you'll probably find that the anger was caused more by misperceptions resulting from fatigue than by reality. The resulting change in perception will instantly lower the feeling of anger, perhaps eliminate it entirely.

Feelings Can Occur in Combination

If the event was actually unfair, however, you need to stop what you're doing and go about making things more fair. Let's say a clerk at the hardware store sells you a tool, saying this is exactly what you need to do some task. But when you get busy working with the new tool, you find that it doesn't work, because it's the wrong tool for the job. You get angry. The tool should work—the salesperson said it would. You paid good money it. You keep trying, but your efforts are useless, so now you're also frustrated.

If you separate the anger from the frustration, you recognize that the situation is unfair because a clerk you trusted recommended the wrong tool for the job. To make the situation fair, you need to go back to the store and return the tool.

Hopefully, you can get an apology from the clerk and exchange the tool for one that will work. If it doesn't happen that way, you can speak to the manager or the store owner, going as high as you need to for satisfaction. If nothing works, your choices are to continue to be angry with the clerk (who has probably forgotten all about you), or to forgive him or her and move on.

The process is the same for all combinations of feelings: separate out the Primary Feelings, do 1-2-3 and take the action most likely to satisfy your need. By taking these steps, you become your own coach, identifying what needs to be done to create a more fulfilling life.

*Distractors can be either part of the
problem or part of the solution—
it all depends on how you use them.*

Chapter 18

The Wisdom of Distractors

The Secret Language of Feelings was written to give you a blueprint for satisfying your needs, wants and desires. However, there are times when we have to delay satisfying them—sometimes indefinitely. The ability to delay gratification of our needs when necessary due to circumstance is a sign of maturity and can serve us well in all areas of our lives. When we're in this situation, distractors, properly used, can be very helpful.

For our purposes, distractors are defined as anything that you can do that temporarily takes your mind off your uncomfortable feelings. It's important to remember, however, that although distractors can provide temporary relief by taking your attention away from what's bothering you, the feeling and the cause of the feeling still exist within you. That's why **satisfying your feelings should always be Plan A, with the use of distractors being Plan B.**

Unmet needs are the source of a whole range of human

problems. The habit of using distractors instead of satisfying our feelings makes us into addicts, whether workaholics, shopaholics, alcoholics or drug addicts. It turns us into whiners, complainers and blamers.

The pattern of using distractors usually starts early in life. For example, children can learn very early that if they feel bad, they can help themselves feel better by distracting themselves. Parents—often unwittingly—teach this behavior. You probably have seen this scenario yourself. A child falls down and begins to cry, whereupon the well-meaning parent says, "There, there... have a cookie and you'll feel better."

Sure enough, when the child begins to eat the cookie, the crying stops. **The child has just learned how to use distractors, and the pattern learned is: When you feel bad, eat.** Such a pattern almost always continues into adulthood, getting more severe as time goes on, since it takes more and more of the distractor to make the person feel better.

The habitual use of distractors might have been your pattern in the past, but now that you've begun to use the secret language of feelings, you've changed. You're probably much more aware of your feelings and much less likely to mindlessly respond to them by distracting. **Once you've broken the pattern of using distractors in a negative (non-satisfying) way, you can begin to use them in a more useful and mature way.**

Using Distractors in a Positive Way

The key to using distractors in a positive and healthy way is to **make the conscious choice to distract, using a distractor that's not harmful to yourself and/or others.** As noted above, satisfying your feelings should always be Plan A, while distracting (Plan B) should be used as a backup plan. You use your Plan B when, for whatever reason, immediately engaging in a satisfying response is not in your best interest, at least in the short term.

Here's an example that can occur in the workplace. You're in a meeting, and your superior says something to you that's not only inaccurate but also grossly unfair. You feel yourself burning up with anger and you really want to confront your boss in order to address the issue of unfairness (Plan A). But there are other people present and a confrontation would have negative consequences outweighing the benefits. You realize you would be better off to just do some deep breathing (Plan B), until there's a better time and place to address the issue of unfairness.

If you're in a home or work situation where you often need to defer gratification, it's very important that you devise a positive—or at least neutral—Plan B before you need it. That way, you won't find yourself implementing a Plan B that has as many negative implications as fulfilling your initial need in the moment.

Let's say you're angry and you can't do anything at the moment to address the need for fairness. You haven't thought about a Plan B for this situation, so you have to come up with a distractor on the spot. When you're angry, however, you aren't in your best creative mode. Chances are good that what you do in this situation might not be in your own best interest.

Here are some other scenarios to consider. If you're overweight and your habitual response to feeling upset is a strong urge to eat, you'll probably overeat at times of emotional upset, even though it isn't in your own best interest to do so.

If you're a person who has used alcohol to cope with unresolved feelings of anger, you'll want to have a drink when you're angry at someone and you can't do anything about it at the moment. It doesn't matter if you know that drinking really isn't in your best interest. Without a positive or neutral Plan B in mind, it's extremely hard not to revert to old habits.

Creating Plan B in Advance

A good Plan B should be constructed in advance—then when you need it, it will be there for you. This is especially true if you're trying to overcome a bad habit like eating too much or drinking too much. Once you've come up with a positive distractor (or several), it's highly recommended that you write them on a card and carry the card with you. That way, you have a list of possible distractors to choose from when you need them. If you use them whenever you need to delay gratification of needs, they will become a habitual positive response.

Here are some guidelines for the use of Plan B (distractors).

The Wisdom of Distractors

Remember, however, that Plan A is always the first, best choice.

1. Distract only when it's not possible or in your best interest at the time to try and satisfy the feeling. It's not a perfect world where we can instantly satisfy all of our feelings in any given moment.

2. Acknowledge that you're distracting rather than satisfying your needs. Be clear that you'll take appropriate actions (make the satisfying response) when the situation allows.

3. Plan to use a distractor that's pleasant and positive, so that you're likely to use it again if need be. (Just about anything on your list for satisfying responses for bored will work.)

4. Don't use a distractor that's illegal, immoral or otherwise not in your best interests.

As you can see, the positive use of distractors requires both a firm understanding of the principles in this book and a willingness to be completely honest with ourselves.

We have to take the time to be aware of our feelings and the needs associated with them. We have to know how to identify a satisfying response and take the action necessary. We also have to be able to recognize those situations where taking positive action isn't in our best interest. We have to be willing, in such cases, to defer gratification by using pre-arranged distractors in a positive way. In other words, we have to be willing to act in a mature and adult fashion.

It takes a lot of courage to do all of the above. But the reward is having a life that's satisfying. One of the main problems in our society with regard to addictions and compulsions, etc. is that the people who engage in these kinds of behaviors think that they are taking care of their problems (emotions). However, they are merely coping with or managing their emotions rather than satisfying them.

Finally, it bears repeating that the distractors we turn to when we can't immediately satisfy our needs should not have any unhealthy consequences. Using drugs to distract, for example, is not only unhealthy, it's illegal in some cases. Any unhealthy or illegal distractor only adds stress and increases the drive to manage through the heightened use of the distractor, a sure cycle of despair.

Even healthy, positive activities, when used to avoid handling the Primary Feeling through positive action, can become unhealthy distractors. Using food as a distractor is the gateway to obesity. Using sex to distract can lead to STDs and broken relationships. Working long hours, jogging compulsively or even immersing yourself in church work can distract, but the effects can be quite negative.

Recommended distractors are any healthy activities that you find pleasant or enjoyable. These are things that you may enjoy that are not illegal, immoral or fattening. For a list of positive distractors, see the list of positive activities in Chapter 6, The Wisdom of Feeling Bored. Then create a list of your own. Just make sure the activities on it are pleasant and harmless.

How Plans A and B Work Together

Let's summarize what we've been talking about. When our "bad" feelings speak to us, they tell us that our life is lacking in some way. The first thing we need to do is to check our perceptions, because sometimes there only seems to be a deficiency. Our initial reaction to a situation may be that it's unfair, but later, we may realize it does have some element of fairness. However, when something is definitely lacking, and some need, want or desire is not being fulfilled, we can thank our inner wisdom for making us feel the painful emotion, which motivates us to act.

Because we understand the secret language of feelings, we know that the name of the feeling indicates the cause of the feeling. Sadness indicates loss, for example. When we know the cause, we also know what we need to do in order to provide for ourselves and others. This provides us with a sense of direction in life, both in the long and short term. ***Fulfilling our needs is Plan A. Whenever our feelings communicate to us that our life is lacking, it's a call to action: Do 1-2-3 self-coaching.***

But sometimes we need to delay gratification of our needs, wants and desires, because for one reason or another they cannot be immediately satisfied. Or perhaps attempting to satisfy a feeling at a particular time may have undesirable consequences. In this case we need a Plan B. ***Our Plan B is a carefully considered set of distractors, healthy ways of taking our minds off the problem until we can take care of it.***

This is just the opposite from how people manage their lives and emotions when they don't understand the secret language of feelings. Most people are living lives of continuous distraction. They are, in effect, consistently choosing to implement Plan B in a negative way, unaware that they have any other option. This leads to a life of constant dissatisfaction and habitual distraction, usually called bad habits, addictions and compulsions. You now have the knowledge and skills to choose a different path, one that leads to a life of fulfillment and satisfaction.

Chapter 19

Creating Positive Programming

For Christmas awhile back, some friends of mine gave me a sweatshirt with the message "Life is Good." When I asked them where they got the idea to put that statement on the sweatshirt, they said, "You're always saying, 'Life is good!'" My response was, "Really?" I'd been saying that for so long, I'd stopped being aware that I was doing it. It had become part of my unconscious programming. Unfortunately, most of us are doing the same thing, except that the programming is much less optimistic.

Here are some examples of the sorts of things people say to themselves over and over again, reinforcing unconscious programming without even realizing it:

> Things never seem to work out for me.
> What can go wrong will go wrong.
> I have a Type A personality.
> I never have enough money.

I'll always be poor.
I always get nervous when I have to take a test.
Every time I try to think positively, something goes wrong.
I can't get out of bed in the morning.
I never get around to exercising.
I'll never get ahead, because people are prejudiced.
I can't help it. I have a bad temper. (I can't manage money, I can never get to places on time, etc.)

There are infinite variations on statements such as these. You could have some fun filling out the following with what comes to mind first—it will probably be the very thing you keep telling yourself about yourself.

I'm too young (too old, too tired, too busy)
to _____.

I can't help it. I have _____.

I can't help it. I just never _____.

No doubt some statements on this list hit home—we all have them inside our heads, running like an endless tape. If you're reading this book, you're someone who is interested in creating a better life, so you have probably tried to stop thinking these negative or fearful thoughts in the past, with little or only temporary success.

That isn't surprising. What most people don't know is that the moment you try to stop thinking those kinds of thoughts, you put yourself in a situation where it's difficult, if not impossible, to stop.

Creating Positive Programming

This concept is so important, I'll repeat it: ***It's very difficult to stop thinking of something if you try to stop thinking of it.***

For example, right now I want you to stop thinking of purple bananas. Come on, try harder. Stop thinking of purple bananas! No more purple bananas!

By now, your mind is probably full of thoughts and images of purple bananas. The fact is, the harder you try to stop thinking about purple bananas, the more you have to think about purple bananas—even if you have never, ever thought about such a thing before.

This exercise illustrates one of the problems people have when they try to stop smoking or drinking. They try not to think about it. They may even say, "I'm not going to think about having a cigarette anymore." That doesn't work. As you have just discovered, the more you try not to think about something, the more you think about it.

The same scenario holds true when the issue is snacking between meals. If you constantly give yourself the suggestion or affirmation that you will *not* snack between meals, you're constantly sending the idea of snacking into your consciousness. The more you try not to think about snacking (or tell yourself you aren't going to think about snacking), the more you do think about it. Constant thoughts of food start the digestive system working, and that makes you feel as if you need to eat, even though you aren't experiencing true physical hunger.

How many times have you said to yourself, "I'm not going to do (fill in an unwanted behavior) anymore." How successful were you at changing your behavior by talking to yourself that way? Probably not very successful. There is a school of thought that says the right brain doesn't hear negatives. If that is so, what are you actually hearing when you say, "I'm not going to yell at my kids."? Your left brain hears that exact phrase, but your right brain hears, "I'm going to yell at my kids." That sets up an internal conflict, which intensifies your struggle with the behavior you want to change. Clearly, a more effective strategy is needed.

Turning Negatives into Positives

At various points in this book, I've suggested practices (**1-2-3** self-coaching and 7th Path™ Self-Hypnosis®) and therapies (5-PATH™ hypnotherapy, Rapid Eye Technology, and the Emotional Freedom Techniques) that are effective for releasing emotions and beliefs rooted in the past. In addition to those approaches, you can begin working on consciously changing your thought patterns. You can construct positive thoughts that reinforce the new, positive beliefs you're choosing.

When you're constructing these positive thoughts, avoid negative words like "don't," "not" and "never." The problem with using these words is that they are always in sentences that reinforce the negative. For example, "I am safe and secure" works much better than "I am not afraid." The phrase, "I am not afraid" reinforces being afraid.

Creating Positive Programming

The positive sentences you create for yourself will reflect the kind of life you would like to be experiencing. By creating them, you're creating an image of that life. Once you have them in mind, whenever habitual negative thoughts arise—and they will, it's how the brain functions—you can replace them with positive expressions of who you are and the life you want to have. Do that often enough and you'll find the old habitual thoughts dissolving and new, positive thoughts taking their place.

Here are some suggestions to get you started:

I am loveable. I am capable. I enjoy my life.
I am a calm and patient parent.
I am keeping up on my studies, and I like that!
I am enjoying wonderful relationships.
I like getting up in the morning and exercising.

Believe it or not, doing this can begin to make a real difference in your life. You can increase the effectiveness of your positive self-statements by using them before you go to sleep at night. When you close your eyes, create a fantasy reflecting the content of the positive self-statement. Feel how it feels being there, especially how good it feels to be experiencing the kind of life you have been longing for. The more pleasurable the fantasy, the better. You're creating a new memory—and your mind doesn't know the difference between it and a memory from your past!

It might take awhile before you start noticing a change in the kind of thoughts your mind cycles through your awareness, but if you add this practice to what you have learned in this book, you will be well on your way to creating a life you will love.

*Now that the Secret Language of Feelings
has been revealed, you can take charge
of your own life—and help others as well.*

Afterword

Going Forward with the Secret Language

You have learned a great deal by reading *The Secret Language of Feelings*, but knowledge is not power. ***Implementation of knowledge is power.*** I encourage you to begin now, if you have not already done so, to use what you've learned in your daily life. If you let it permeate your thinking, it will utterly change you, making you into the kind of person you've longed to be. You'll be aware of what you're feeling; aware of what you need, want and desire; and able to take appropriate action to create a satisfying life, free of the problems that brought you to this book.

Because you understand the secret language of feelings, boredom becomes a call for achievement. Sadness becomes a call for reclamation. Loneliness, a call for relationship building. Anger, a motivation for achieving fairness or forgiveness. Frustration, a call for creativity. And depression, a call for rest until you're ready to try again. By heeding the call, you'll become a person who achieves more, is happier and has many satisfying relationships. You'll become a problem solver, who understands that the world is a place filled with hope.

One result of understanding and practicing the **1-2-3** of the secret language is compassion. You'll begin to realize that if the information contained in this book is true for you, it's also true for others. You'll recognize what others are feeling and what needs are unsatisfied. This gives you a greater understanding of people, compassion for their suffering and patience with their struggle to make their lives work.

Now, I know there are some of you who have read this book from cover to cover, yet are still wondering if the secret language will be able to help you improve the quality of your life. You may be thinking, "I really want to believe I can change, but I'm afraid it's too late for me. I have too much baggage. Nothing I have ever tried has made a difference." To you, I'd like to say, "Take hope." Sincere study and application of the secret language of feelings will improve anyone's life.

Others may be thinking, "I can see how **1-2-3** works with what I'm feeling in the present, but how do I get rid of all those painful feelings from the past? How do I get rid of anger, sadness and depression? How do I get rid of addiction?" Again I say, "Take hope." You can change. You can be successful. You can be happy. You can live up to your potential.

There are techniques specifically designed to help you rapidly

Afterword

take care of the old feelings blocking your way to freedom and happiness, among them Rapid Eye Technology and Emotional Freedom Techniques. If you work with one of these techniques while also doing your ongoing practice of **1-2-3,** you'll move through any perceived blocks to expressing your full potential.

One such process that I admire, Universal Therapy, is taught by Gerald F. Kein. At our center we offer two programs that were influenced both by his teachings and personal experience conducting thousands of hypnosis sessions. They are 5-PATH™ hypnotherapy and 7th Path™ Self-Hypnosis, a holistic, mind-body-spirit approach to ongoing self-improvement. (See appendix for more information about 5-PATH™, 7th Path™ and Universal Therapy.)

Regardless of where you are on the path to a more satisfying life, you can move forward. You now have a powerful tool to help you along the way. And you can use that tool to help others.

If you're a parent, use what you've learned to create a better relationship with your children. Teach them how to use the **1-2-3** of the secret language to handle the upsets of childhood and adolescence.

If you're a helping professional, doctor, psychologist, counselor, manager or supervisor, use the secret language of feelings in your professional work with others. You'll offer them the key to understanding an important part of their humanity—and a tool to affect change.

If you're a teacher or coach, apply this information as you interact with your students. Teach them the secret language and **1-2-3** as a technique for problem solving and conflict resolution.

All of us—parents, instructors, and helping professionals—teach best by example. As you reflect on what you've learned and begin using **1-2-3** self-coaching as an ongoing practice, others will notice you have become calmer and are leading a more successful and satisfying life.

Imagine the difference it will make to have more and more people experiencing that sort of change! Earlier in this book, I wrote about how habitual stress and fear can be learned and passed down from generation to generation. The good news is that positive patterns—using our understanding of emotions to build a satisfying life—can also be learned and passed down.

You're now part of a small revolution that can make a big difference!

If you're interested in additional training or information on this material, I invite you to contact the publisher or visit our web site (see appendix).

Calvin D. Banyan, MA

Appendix

A Brief Description of 5-PATH® Hypnotherapy

5-PATH® hypnotherapy and 7th Path Self-Hypnosis® is a brief therapy where issues are usually worked through in about six sessions. If you decide to connect with a specially trained 5-PATH® Hypnotherapist, you will meet one-on-one with him or her in private sessions. This professional knows how to use the secret language of feelings and hypnosis to help you get past the blockages that are in the way of your success.

A Brief Description of 7th Path Self-Hypnosis®

Some people prefer to do their personal work using a technique or practice such as 7th Path Self-Hypnosis®. This new form of self-hypnosis is one of the things that I am most proud of. It is a mind-body-spirit approach that enables you to remove the old programming and replace it with positive suggestions that will set you free to really be successful in your life.

One of the wonderful things about the 7th Path™ system is that you can work on all of your issues or concerns in the privacy of your own mind! You don't have to talk about your problems with a therapist if you do not want to. This is a wonderful way for private individuals to benefit from our program. It is also a practical alternative if there is no 5-PATH® trained hypnotherapist near where you live.

The Secret Language of Feelings

There are three ways to learn and benefit from 7th Path Self-Hypnosis®. The first is to work with a professional one-on-one. In this case, you do get personal instruction, but you need not talk about your past at all, so there is still a degree of privacy around your personal issues. Usually you can learn enough to use the system in about three to five sessions.

The second way is to attend a 7th Path Self-Hypnosis® class. These workshops allow individuals who feel comfortable in a classroom/workshop environment to learn the system in as few as one or two days.

The third way is to study 7th Path™ is through the home-study course, which is a recorded version of the 7th Path™ workshops. Some of our students like to have both live training and the recorded versions for practice and review. For more information, visit the 7th Path Self-Hypnosis® website at http://www.7thpath-selfhypnosis.com

Training Opportunities

If you are a helping professional who would like to train to become a hypnotherapist, or if you are interested in a change of careers, contact us and learn about our training programs or a similar program near you. We have accelerated programs that may fit into your schedule. People who do not have advanced degrees are eligible for training and certification in hypnotherapy.

Appendix

For More Information

You can learn more about the secret language of feelings, 5-PATH® hypnotherapy and 7th Path Self-Hypnosis® by visiting our websites at http://www.hypnosiscenter.com and http://www.7thPathSelfHypnosis.com. It features a directory of 5-PATH® hypnotherapists and 7th Path™ teachers, free articles on hypnosis and hypnotherapy and links to other hypnotherapy schools, organizations and professionals.

If you have questions or wish to order individual copies or wholesale quantities of this book, go to our website listed above or contact our office at:

Banyan Hypnosis Center for Training & Services, Inc.
275 West Campbell Rd., Suite 245
North Dallas, Texas 75080
U.S.A.

<u>**Tel:**</u> 469-969-2176 or   Toll Free: 800-965-3390

<u>**Email:**</u> CustomerService@hypnosiscenter.com

Banyan Hypnosis Center for Training & Services, Inc. also publishes "Hypnosis and Hypnotherapy: Basic to Advanced Techniques for the Professional" by Calvin D. Banyan and Gerald F. Kein, and also "Real Hypnosis Business Success" by Calvin D. Banyan et al.

Index

Index